THE PROPHET:

A TRAGEDY.

BY

BAYARD TAYLOR,

AUTHOR OF "LARS," "THE MASQUE OF THE GODS," ETC., ETC.

BOSTON:
JAMES R. OSGOOD AND COMPANY,
(LATE TICKNOR & FIELDS, AND FIELDS, OSGOOD, & CO.)
1874.

STEREOTYPED AND PRINTED BY
RAND, AVERY, AND COMPANY, BOSTON.

THE PROPHET.

DRAMATIS PERSONÆ.

DAVID STARR	*The Prophet*
ELKANAH	*His Father*
HANNAH	*His Mother*
RHODA	*Afterwards his Wife*
NIMROD KRAFT	*Afterwards High Priest*
LIVIA ROMNEY	*A Woman of the World*
SIMEON, MORDECAI, HUGH, JONAS	*Members of the Council of Twelve*
SARAH	*Wife of Jonas*
PETER	*An Orphan, the Prophet's Serving-Man*
COLONEL HYDE	*Sheriff*
HIRAM	*A Member of the Church*

A Preacher. People of David's neighborhood. Members of the church. Women. Colonel Hyde's followers.

Time, 18—.

The scene of Act I. is a New-England State; of the four following Acts, a Western State.

Between Acts I. and II. there is an interval of two years; between Acts II. and III., an interval of one year.

THE PROPHET.

ACT I.

Scene I.

The porch, front-yard, and garden of a farm-house. Late afternoon.

ELKANAH

'Tis a good ending of the harvest. Now
We may be sure that every sheaf is stacked
Ere rain can spoil it. "One load more, I think,"
Said David. But the farther side is low,
A deeper soil, bears well: he may be wrong,
If on the right side of the estimate.
I always counted less than likely seemed;
Tried to surprise myself, as it might be,

And so increase my luck. He's over young
For under-guessing; takes the most at once,
And discounts profit long before it comes.
The lad is not like me, or times are changed.
I was my father over, he declared,
And liked to say so; but good stock improves;
Hey, Hannah?

HANNAH

Nay, I heard you: I must think,
Whether I will or no, about the boy,
As in the anxious time when he was born.
Late fruit is best, they say, — the only kind
Keeps over winter; but it may get ripe,
Like pippins, when the orchard's bare of leaves.
Your disappointment and your discontent
You do forget; but I remember all,
Bearing the blame: and when he came, at last,
I said within my heart, Because of that

The Lord means something. Now I plague myself,
Thinking I see, and straightway seeing not,
The sign thereof revealed in David's life.

ELKANAH

You could not help such fancies, I suppose,
While he was on the way.

HANNAH

I know your thought:
You've the same right to seek yourself in him,
But will not find it: he is most of me.
Why, forty years have you and I been wed;
And four and twenty has he been with us.
I cannot say beforehand, thus and so
Will speak my husband, or decide, or act;
But I must wait: yet, if a woman were
By some strange miracle become a man,
Then I should be our David's very self
In feeling and in purpose. Something moves

His mind beyond our daily round of work:
I know not what it is, and dare not ask,
Lest prying words, before the proper time,
Breed mischief.

ELKANAH

Wife, the boy is all a man:
He'll soon spy out what's wanting.

HANNAH

Ah, not that!

PETER

(*Singing at a distance.*)

Sing, blow the wind o' mornings!
Sing, blow the wind, 'igh O!
Sing, brush away the morning dew,
Sing, blow, blow, blow!

ELKANAH

The last load: otherwise, would Peter sing
Not quite so loudly. They have built it broad,
Mayhap, and high, to save another. Well,

Whether it show good luck or management
Makes odds in the end. There be two ways of
work;
And one is doing it because you must,
And one because you like. Look when it's done,
You'll see small difference, as the case is now;
And I misdoubt me sorely which it is.

DAVID

(Singing, distant at first, but gradually drawing nearer.)

If one to yonder mountain saith,
Be cast into the sea!
And doubteth not, so filled with faith,
The mount removed shall be.
Though love is first, yet faith is chief:
Lord, I believe; help Thou mine unbelief!

Behold, He granteth prophecy,
And gift of tongues, to all:
His fullest bounty waits for me,
Though I delay to call.
The measure of our days is brief:
Lord, I believe; help Thou mine unbelief!

[RHODA, *approaching the house from the opposite side, pauses at the gate, and listens. She begins to sing, at first in a low voice, then louder to the close; when* DAVID *appears.*]

DAVID

I thought of you, and straightway find you here.
Was that your prayer, as well? I'll not believe
You utter words, as one lets pebbles drop,
To splash in water: you've a healthful soul,
I think, to make another's faith more firm
By just believing, Rhoda?

RHODA

What I am
Can I declare?

DAVID

Then I will set you forth.
I'll say that love in you is one with faith:

The trust you give means an eternal term,
And following through good and ill report,
And with strong heart sustaining where the mind
Would stop and question. These were woman's
gifts
When she beheld the Master, and obeyed;
And they are yours: if I supposed you false,
I should be most unhappy.

RHODA

No, not false!
Believe me, David, any thing but that!
[*They pass into the garden.*

HANNAH

They both forget us! Even his face is strange,
Most strange and beautiful with serious thought;
While hers is troubled, yet has nought of pain.
I do not understand it. She's a child,

Is Rhoda still; and wise she never seemed.
Can one give counsel, comprehending not
The doubtful matter? Surely unto her
He cannot show what he keeps back from
me!
Men seek clear notions, whether fair or foul,
When they have pondered any thing so long
As he with this. They take the orchard-path.
The fruit will hardly be their chief concern,
Yet gives fair ground that I may follow them.

[*Exit.*

ELKANAH

(*Laughing to himself.*)

Ha, ha! I see no mystery in the thing.
A practised tongue has Hannah, takes her way
And justifies it, past my argument;
Yet now and then, like one in too much haste,
Her notions trip, and throw her flat on mine.

Because the lad was moony, she, forsooth,
Must think him like a Samuel, set apart
For this or t'other; but it's nothing new.
He goes the way of flesh and blood, that first
Knows hardly what the natural ailment is,
Till each finds out, and then the other heals.
Yes, yes, these women! Best to give them line,
And let them pry a while among the clouds
For what their very noses touch. She kept
Him close, and preached upon and coddled him,
As if a root of wilder oats is killed
When you keep down the top. The girl, 'tis true,
Might have a bigger dowry: let that pass!
High time it is to settle him afresh;
And Hannah has no call to interfere.

[*Exit.*

[HANNAH, DAVID, *and* RHODA *return.*]

DAVID

Neither to you nor Rhoda, mother. Both
Must wait what cometh; for, if I could say,
Then I should know.

HANNAH

And each of you is sure
You love the other? I have seen no signs.
Even neighbors' children do not change so much,
But there is seeking, doubt, and bashfulness,
Which will betray them.

DAVID

None of these are ours:
I did not seek what was already found;
And truth in me prohibits doubt of her.
If what concerneth life was once ordained

For others, there must be direction still.
The nearest heart is ever easiest read:
So, reading Rhoda's by the light of mine
And that above, as one may hold pure glass
Before the least of stars, nor make it dim,
I saw that each was chosen. Rhoda, speak,
And tell me once again your heart is mine!

RHODA

You know it, even if I answered Nay.

Scene II. — A Camp-Meeting.

A grove of large, scattered oak-trees. Against two, which stand near together, a platform is built, supporting a pulpit of rough timber. In front of the platform are benches of planks, upon which several hundred persons are seated, David, Rhoda, *and* Peter *among them. Tents are pitched under the borders of the grove. Many persons kneeling at the front benches, weeping and shouting.*

HYMN.

There is a fountain filled with blood,
  Drawn from Immanuel's veins;
And sinners, plunged beneath that flood,
  Lose all their guilty stains.

THE PREACHER

(*Resuming his exhortation, which was interrupted by the hymn.*)

Oh, there are more among ye shall be plucked
As brands from out the burning! By the hair
I'll seize you, — even by the single hair
That holds you from the pit! My hands are singed
With loosening the Devil's grip on souls;
And you, who should strike out with fists and feet,
Leave me the fight, the cowards that you are!
You think the Lord can't see you: even so
The ostrich sticketh in the sand her head
To save her gay tail-feathers: pull them out,

And cast them from you! Though you hide
 yourselves
Under the mountains, it will not be long;
He'll send you wriggling forth, as mean as mice:
And, though you dive down in the deepest sea,
He'll haul you to the surface like a whale,
Harpooned, and spouting blood.

[*Cries and groans among the people.*]

Yes, gnash and roar
Like lions on the hills of Havilum;
But, all the same, He'll ask full price of you.
Come up, ye publicans and sinners! Kneel,
Pray hard, mourn with the mourners, and be
 saved!
Strike off the crusted brimstone from your feet,
And swap the Devil's fire for water of life!
Oh! don't I know you? This one's pride of mind,
And that one's wretched fear of what folks say,

And t'other's cold "morality," as if
An ice-house better than an oven baked, —
Oh! don't I know? I had them all myself:
I was a scurvy sheep, distempered, bad
With foot and mouth disease: He picked me up,
And, as it were, greased me with oil of grace,
And washed my spotted fleece until it shone.
You think you're clean already; but He sees
Red under broadcloth, silk, and calico, —
Only your livers white!

[*Several more come forward to the front benches, and kneel down with loud cries.*]

Two, three, four, five!
Each one as nine and ninety righteous men:
Why, these alone outweigh the rest of you!
You give a serpent when he asks for fish;
And He upsets, as men their wagons tilt,
His four-horse loads of mercies and of gifts,

And buries with them all that say, "I need."

[*His eyes meet those of* DAVID, *who leans forward in his seat with a fixed, abstracted gaze.*]

I see another sinner! He's afraid:
It may be that he magnifies his sin.
But, don't you know, the bigger load you bear,
The greater comfort when you cast it off?
Oh! you'll be pardoned fully, not a doubt:
He likes to pardon. Trembling brother, come!
You will not? Say, then, do you love the Lord?

DAVID

(*Rising, as if with a struggle, and speaking slowly.*)

Whether I love Him, and how well, He knows.

PETER

(*Aside to his neighbor.*)

Not quite the answer he expected.

THE PREACHER

Yes,
He knoweth. Do you seek a hole in the net,
Caught by the gills already? Yes, He knows:
These mourners cry to Him because of that.

DAVID

Let Him be Judge of me!

THE PREACHER

He is your Judge
Without your letting. These are Devil's tricks, —
This playing pitch-and-toss with holy words,
To gain a little time. Come up, choose sides!
The Lord means business. Where a gnat's enough
For others, must you have an elephant,
And all His promises rammed down your throat,
Before you know their taste?

DAVID

(*Eagerly.*)

His promises?—
The power of miracle and prophecy,
And gift of tongues? He promised them to all;
And Paul confirmed it. Tell me, then, the signs!
The heart within me aches from stress of faith:
I have no need to pray, except for power,
Which is the seal and covenant for them
Whom He has chosen.

[*Movements and exclamations among the people.*

THE PREACHER

So take hold on hell
The proud of spirit. What! the gift of tongues,
The power of miracle and prophecy,
You ask, without repentance, prayer, and grace?

DAVID

For what should I repent? Why pray as these
Who cry from secret consciousness of sin?
I never let a fault against me stand
For day of settlement, then balanced all
By pleading bankrupt, only to begin
A fresh account. Acceptance, yea, and faith,
Are mine already, tenfold more than yours,
Who neither ask, nor know what ye should ask.

THE PREACHER

We choose His simple way. You would mislead:
Be silent!

CRIES AMONG THE PEOPLE

Out! A very infidel! —
No sinner? Never prays? Why, Antichrist
Could say no more! To face the preacher so!
Away with him!

PETER

(Turning suddenly, with clinched fists.)

The preacher drew him on,
And got no worse than he deserved. I say,
Touch him, it won't be "Glory!" that you'll shout,
After a sore repentance.

DAVID

If I shake
This dust from off my feet, I do no more
Than was commanded. Have you privilege
To darken counsel with your cloud of words?
To teach the lesser part, reject the whole,
And mutilate His glory unto men?
Woe to the Pharisees and hypocrites,
Even here as there, even in these latter days,
As when upon the paths of Galilee
His feet were beautiful! My words are said.

[*He leaves the place amid a great outcry and confusion.*

SCENE III.

A lonely lane, evening.

DAVID

(*Solus.*)

Cast out? By them that think they do believe,
Cursed for believing? God! what, then, is truth?
Why, here Thy minted gold is worn with use,
Sweated in handling, till the head thereon
Is quite rubbed out, the superscription dim.
I did but offer it as freshly coined,
With all its glorious promise legible,
And they cry, "Counterfeit!" Ten talents given,
Nine have they buried, and a single one
Divide among the people, who are blind,
And blindly led: shall I not therefore see?

[*He pauses, and looks upwards.*]

How reach the faith so perfect and assured
That every gift must follow? I have tried,

Sought evidence in lightest, easiest ways:
Nothing obeyed. So I have *not* the faith,
Or— O my God! there is no faith, no power,
Nor miracle; and never can have been.
But this is madness! This makes truth a lie,
Makes life an emptiness far worse than death,
Peoples the world with devils, drives men mad,
And substitutes—

[*Another pause.*]

I had not thought of that.
Times changed, conditions changed: hence special need
Of worthiness through trial, harder now
Than when all understood what meant belief,
And perfect faith was natural to them.
How can I measure mine by other men's?
I saw not right: I claimed the highest power,
Unpurchased. What apostle shall declare,

As then, the fealty of a human soul?
Not he; not he! And are not all alike,
Giving their husks of doctrine for His bread?
The ground we stand on is too far apart:
Whom seek? Why, none! A hand is on my head,
A finger points the way.

PETER

(*Coming up.*)

I meant to leave
When you did; but, because I cannot swear
As properly as they, and just let fly
Hard lumps of words like stones to hit and hurt,
They cursed me roundly, — in a holy way;
And one, with hand upon my collar, cried,
"Down, sinner, and repent!" I answered him
Between the eyes; then dashed the rest apart,
And so got headway. Let us hurry on:
They're after us.

DAVID

And if they were? My right
Is greater. Did you understand my words?

PETER

As much as his. He did not answer you:
That I could understand.

DAVID

If unto you
So much was manifest, and to the rest,
They only want authority and sign,
Which I must purchase. Peter, I believe
All men are brethren when they see the truth.

PETER

You never called me "brother;" yet you did
Even as a brother.

DAVID

Did I so, indeed?
I thought not of it.

[*They walk forwards.*]

PETER

Why should you not preach?
There always must be preachers in the world.
We're used to them; and people say that things
Would go to wrack without them; but I wish
They'd yell and bang and thunder less. Somehow
The text is friendly, smooth, and innocent
As seems a flint; yet soon they knock from it
Thick sparks of hell-fire; and the sulphur-stink
Goes to men's heads, and sets them raving wild.
You'd preach some comfort, now.

DAVID

Would you believe?

PETER

Why not? Something we must believe, they say.
What I can't understand I take on trust.
It's getting late: the hogs and cattle know
There's earlier feeding-time when Sunday comes.

[He hastens on.

DAVID

The world is peaceful. There should be no sin:
There need not be, or misery, any more.
Yon blue is loftier than the changing wind,
And spreads serenely back of cloud and storm
To show us what we might be. Wherefore strive?
Faith puts contention quietly aside,
Smiles, and is master.

[Rhoda overtakes him.]

I have need of you,
My Rhoda. Sooner than the signs announced,

The time draws nigh. Here, walk beside me now
At the beginning, as it were the end.

RHODA

I was not frightened. All you said was true.
I thought you answered as one having power;
And so did many others.

DAVID

Rhoda, look!
How yonder little cloud is all afire,
As if a rose unshrivelled so could burn,
That was so gray and dull! Even such am I.
I cannot help the color, nor escape
The light that shines upon me. You will be
Yon other cloud, that mingles with the first
While now we gaze; and let the multitude
Spread as the clammy meadow-mists below,
That never saw the sunset.

RHODA

And I feared
That you might be disquieted in soul.
Your peace and strength leave all the trouble mine.
I can but take whatever light is yours,
That is not wasted from a nobler use.
I will not speak of mine unworthiness;
For that were thankless censure of your heart,
Which finds me worthy.

DAVID

Proven so again!
You are a glass wherein I see myself
Reflected as I change, — now clear, now dim,
And soon (or else, I think, the earth shall cease)
Clothed on with brightness, as a lamp with flame.

RHODA

I pray that I may read what you intend.
It must be so: how, otherwise, give help?

DAVID

Will help be needed?

RHODA

Will not trouble come?
I have the feeling that foretells a storm
When not a cloud has gathered, — sultry, strange.
And full of restlessness which is not fear.
This is of me alone: untouched are you
By that which you regard not.

DAVID

Let me be!
Stand off, keep silence, wait and hope! One step
Gives me the pathway; but my lifted foot
Feels in the dark, conjectures an abyss

Where one bold thrust might touch the solid base.
My peace and strength, you said? There's seem
ing peace
When hope, desire, and prayer have done their
most,
And wait in agony the answer. Come!
I hardly feel the earth that bears me up.
The sky is blazing; all the air is gold;
And every hill-top is a step to heaven.

[*They pass on.*

Scene IV.

The sitting-room of the farm-house, dusk. Hannah *seated in an old arm-chair at the window.*

HANNAH

If half of Peter's story be the truth,
The thing will make disturbance. Not of that,
As him affecting, should I be afraid,
Were not the place, and manner of his words,

Weapons against him. Brooding men are rash
When forced or cozened to declare themselves;
And he has made, if more his thought includes,
Unwise beginning. Whither will it lead?
He angers me, who, in my younger days,
Was often hotly angered with myself
Without such bitter cause; and, having led
In love so long, I now must lead by blame.
It is a pestilent business, and for nought!
I did not say a word against his choice,
Though higher — he a man so proper, she
As hundreds are — he had the right to look.
And now this useless, flighty piece of work!

ELKANAH

(*Entering.*)

Oh, yes! you've heard. Although I hardly see
Your face, I know you know it. Well, this once
I think we shall agree.

HANNAH

First speak your mind.

ELKANAH

My mind is yours. I always thought you wise
As women may be: therefore there's no cause
To make this that, when all is clear as day.
My name and standing in the neighborhood,
And yours, are likely to be touched; for none
Will side with him.

HANNAH

How? None? Suppose him right,
Not rash or flighty, as the thing may seem,
But wise and well-considered, shall he bear
Unjust abuse, and we take no concern?
Then were our name and standing touched in-
deed!

ELKANAH

(*Lifting up his hands.*)

Why, wedded forty years (the words are yours),
I cannot say beforehand, thus and so
Will speak my wife, when wisdom, reason sense,
Have but one language. Did I call you wise?
I knew not what I said. The moon-struck boy
First cracks the egg-shell of his addled brain;
And yours, to please him, then begins to split.

HANNAH

Elkanah, hush! But, nay! speak as you list,
And let your anger breathe itself on me.
Though I be sore confounded, I withhold
Untimely chiding, which confirms the fault
Not felt as such by him; and, if the thing
Be verily justified, avoid a sin.
Be gentle with your first and only born.

DAVID

(Entering hastily.)

Father! Mother!

HANNAH

Behold us here, my son!

DAVID

I will not call you any other names,
Though all be granted.

ELKANAH

As a favor, then?
Say more, or less, and let your riddles drop.
My wits are dumb.

DAVID

This *must* be the command.

[*Exit.*

ELKANAH

If ever! Did you mark his lordly air?
Let us be thankful, that, because he made

A strange disturbance in a godly place,
He still acknowledges he is our son.

HANNAH

(*Rising.*)

Oh, spare me any more! 'Twas not in pride
He spake. He scarcely thought of us: his soul
Is moved by madness, or a mighty truth,
Or both in battle. All my blood grew cold:
My limbs are trembling still.

[*She lights a lamp.*]

I fear the dusk.
There was a bat before the window brushed,
A hoot-owl cried. Well, call me any thing—
Mistaken, silly, weak—when this is past;
But now be kind.

[DAVID *comes back. He pauses in the centre of the room, with a strange, rapt expression of face.*]

Will you not speak to us,
My son? Declare so much as may be told.
We listen.

DAVID

(As if speaking to himself.)

Quarantania!

HANNAH

(After a pause.)

Nay, nay, nay,
This is no answer: do not frighten us!
Whatever purpose so disturbs your brain
You cannot speak it, neither shape its form
Clearly unto yourself, give words, but words:
Silence is poison.

DAVID

(Louder than before.)

Quarantania!

[He passes out the door.

HANNAH

Ah,

He's lost! My husband, help! the world is dark.

[*She falls in a swoon.*

Scene V.

A wild, rocky valley between hills covered with forests; on the left an overhanging cliff; a small brook in the foreground.

DAVID

(*Solus.*)

The second day is sinking to its end,
How slowly! These eternities of thought
Wherein I grope, and strive to lose myself,
Spin to a weary length the glaring hours.
I would the night were come; for I am faint;
And from my hold the things I pray to reach
Seem weakly slipping. Night will give them back,
When every star shines comfort, and the air

Is crossed all ways by print of noiseless feet
That on mysterious errands come and go.
Could I recall my vision! All is clear
Save that — my bed of leaves beneath the rock;
The doubt if I were still indeed myself,
And any thing was what it seemed; until
Came languid peace, then awe and shuddering
Without a cause, a frost in every vein,
And the heart hammered, as to burst mine ears:
Something slid past me, cold and serpent-like:
The trees were filled with whispers; and afar
Called voices not of man: and then my soul
Went forth from me, and spread and grew aloft
Through darting lights — His arrows here and there
Shot down on earth. But now my knowledge fades:
What followed, keener, mightier, than a dream,
My hope interprets. Only this I know, —

The dark, invisible pillars of the sky
Breathed like deep organ-pipes of awful sound:
A myriad myriad tongues the choral sang;
And drowned in it, stunned with excess of power,
My soul sank down, and sleep my body touched.

[*He pauses, and looks around.*]

The shadows will not lengthen. All my throat
Seems choked with dust. I never knew before
How beautiful may be a little brook.
I cannot leave it, cannot turn mine eyes,
So tempting and so innocent it runs.
If I might drink! The dry blood else may breed
Fever and flightiness. I must be sound,
Or soon —

[*He stoops suddenly, dips up the water in his hand, and drinks.*]

Oh, sweet as Cana's wedding-wine!
Did He not offer it? Such sudden bliss,

Born of the body, penetrates my brain!
I doubt no more: the vision will return.

[*There is a rustling among the leaves. A snake thrusts its head forth from under a bush, and gazes at him.*]

Temptation, was it? and the tempter, thou,
In thy first shape? I will not be afeared.
If thou hast power, come forth: if I, depart!
I dare the fascination of thine eyes.
Look thou, lest mine subdue thee. Is it so?
He veils the glittering, bead-like sparks, and turns,
Startled, and winds in sinuous escape.
Why, this is fresh fulfilment of the Word!
Faint not, my soul: the rest will surely come.

[*He walks slowly away.*

(*After a little space enters*)

NIMROD KRAFT

Yon must be he they seek: he is the same
I also seek; but let me not be rash.

If, by the spirit driven that bade him speak,
He hides for meditation, or is verily daft,
As they whose minds take up too sore a load,
He must be humored. I will watch him close
Until some act or gesture give me hint,
And then approach discreetly.

[*He follows.*

(*Enter* RHODA *and* PETER.)

PETER

Shall I call
(He knows my whoop), or sing the hymn he made?

[*Sings, but not loudly.*]

"If one to yonder mountain saith,
'Be cast into the sea!'"

There! I forget the rest.

RHODA

Nay, now; keep still!
I've but a guess to guide me; and it says

He will not see us. Sure, that word betrayed
His thought. But can this be the place? or
where?
Ah, while we wait, perhaps he's lying dead!
Foolish! I know he lives. Some lives are safe,
Because they are not meant for pleasant paths:
Some wits keep sound, to work for other minds.
I must not fear; he would not have me fear:
If he discover us, I must be shamed,
Showing so little faith.

PETER

And so much care!
If this goes on, I'll shortly preach myself.
I'll give you sparrows for example, toads,
And stupid owls: no one goes off alone,
And t'other fears to look for't! Did the Lord
Put such a powerful pressure on his head,

To leave him, sudden, like a will-o'-the-wisp,
The work unfinished? Then 'twas not the Lord.

RHODA

You've spoken wiselier, Peter, than you think.

PETER

So wisdom's cheap! I never valued much
My random notions: what they call horse-sense
I always had; and that sometimes will serve
Even folks that prance so high above our heads.
Now, here's the question: Is he like to starve?
You think he means to try it. Well and good!—
And we must search, but not find openly;
Feed him, without his knowledge; watch his ways,
And not be noticed. So I've nought to do
But look for tracks, and leave the provender:
The risk is yours.

[*He goes slowly up the brook, with a basket on his arm.*

RHODA

(*Solus.*)

I try to force my soul
To follow his, and question not the way.
Within this valley called the Wilderness
He must be hidden, if I understand,
To win, in solitude, the faith and power.
'T s pleasant, now: the shadows of the hills
Soothe the hot leaves with dreams of coming dew;
The crannies of the serpent-haunted rocks
No longer threaten; and the water here
Runs onward with a soft, contented sound.
I will believe him safe. And what is night
But as a darksome cloth that covers us?
Nothing can harm him, for he did no harm;
And that for which he goes apart from all
Will be vouchsafed, or prayer is fruitless breath.

PETER

(*Returning.*)

I found his track! — beside yon biggest rock,
On the flat sand, a little water-soaked,
And made so freshly, that I stooped. You said
He must not see us.

RHODA

And you left him food?

PETER

Upon a shelf that jutted from the rock,
Smooth as a platter. There's no other place,
Up stream or down, but briery thickets grow;
And, if he pass before the fowls o' the air
Spy out his supper —

RHODA

Come, it is enough!
So glad am I at having guessed aright,

I crave no more, lest, pressing on too close,
I spoil the certainty of what remains.

[*Exeunt.*

Scene VI.

Another part of the valley; Nimrod Kraft *near some bushes;* David *at a little distance.*

NIMROD

Behind these bushes I can watch at will.
He thinks himself alone; nay, not of that
Thinks he at all: his gaze is bent aloft,
Or falls, and roots itself before his feet.
So young! Yet even here he bears himself
As one commissioned, who but waits the brief,
With seal and clear subscription, ere he act.
Why not? Has God been sleeping all this while,
Or only men? They stand afar and strange,
And count their generations Gentile still.
Of Christian parents Christian children come,

Baptized before begotten, then at birth
Set back to ancient heathendom, and spoiled
Of all their hoarded heritage. Not such
Is he: he claims his birthright, will possess,
And may restore to others, bringing back
The old, forgotten forces of the Church,
Whose right hand is Authority, whose left
Obedience. But, however he may build,
My coarser strength must hew and set the stones.
If but my purpose can be squared with his!
Since he has entered in this open tract
His spirit wavers: I can see his lips
Move, as do such that know not if they speak.
There is no better moment: I will go.

[*He steps forth, and approaches* DAVID.]

The soul within me hither turns my feet,
And calls upon you. Guide me, help; forgive
If that my haste offend! I come as he,

Lame from his birth, that shouted, leapt, and ran,
When once the gentle touch had made him whole.

DAVID

(After a pause.)

I healed you, then, not knowing.

NIMROD

Marvel not!
There's too much virtue in a perfect faith
To take the measure of itself. You ARE;
And what you are, not knowing, is the power.

DAVID

Nay, there! What I invoke I cannot be.
How know you aught of me?

NIMROD

Yourself did make
The revelation. When I saw your face
Rise from the crowd, I said within my heart,

"There's one will sign his own free covenant!
He reaches high: my arms are short and strong;
But they may touch the gifts within his hand."
You spake. I stood afar; but in my mouth
Came a sweet savor, though their husks and stones
Still harsh and heavy on my stomach sat.
It needs no thousand words to make acquaint:
There's something runs in souls more close than
    blood
Of them that issue from the selfsame womb;
And so in yours. I will not guess your prayer;
But its fulfilment surely is at hand.

DAVID

(*Hastily.*)

Make no conjecture! Speak no further word!
There was a veil within the Temple: grant
I may have lifted up its awful folds,
And stand, not blasted yet, nor consecrate.

NIMROD

So think of me as one that waits without,
Silent, and hoping much. But, ere I go,

[*Kneels.*]

I pray you lay your hands upon my head,
And bless me, wishing that to my belief
Be added understanding; to my will,
The power to serve; to mine obedience,
Some gracious gift.

DAVID

(*Aside.*)

How, then? Without the power
Assume the office? Yet a blessing dwells
Within the heart of him that calls it down;
Or else he dare not.

[*To* NIMROD.]

As thou askest, so
May it be given! From laying here my hands
Expect no unction more than I possess.

NIMROD.

(*Rising.*)

But more than I am worthy to receive
Is even that, so filled am I with light!
And they, dumb souls, who for a single ray
Shout "Glory!" and are saved, — how could
they bear
The flood that enters me from you? Farewell!
A part is granted: you have forced the gate,
And stand with dazzled eyesight. When you see,
Come back to men.

[*Exit.*

DAVID

A powerful soul! and yet
Acknowledges authority in me.
Why was I faint or doubtful? Have I reached
Too high, perchance, or dreamed commissioned
power

Should be by signs and wonders heralded,
Not as the simple consequence of faith?
Faith is as beauty is: no maiden feels
Through inner sense the glory of her face;
But it shines back on her from who perceives.
"With dazzled eyesight"? Darkness comes of that;
And on the finished shrine He sank in cloud.
If power unconsciously be held, I climb
The while I seem to beat a weary round;
Possess authority beyond my sense;
Am blinded, yea, because so near the light;
And weak, since even now my shoulders bear
The unwonted burden. Let the vision come!
It cannot fail: the first and largest star
Already glimmers from the expanding vault;
And millions wait behind. So sure as they
Shall pierce the veil when thickest, even so
The first faint lamp within a seeking soul
Foretells the revelations crowding on.

SCENE VII.

A room in the farm-house; ELKANAH, HANNAH, DAVID, RHODA.

HANNAH

I try to understand you: if I fail,
The heart your baby head found comfort on
Is not to blame.

ELKANAH

It's all a waste of words!
You look for duty, and it's asked of you:
Command, or wish, or plead, one answer comes, —
He has "authority:" so much I've learned.
When once a man says that, you might as soon
Prevail upon a tortoise in the shell:
No words go through it. I have said my say.

DAVID

If I had given you grief of heart ere this,
Sinned unrepenting, disobeyed your will,

What I have done would bring rejoicing now.
There's no perversity in whole desire,
Or the receiving of the gifts unused
Because unclaimed. I could not help but reach;
Then, plucking back my hand, I found it filled.
What said you, mother, all my years of youth,
But "Seek, and ye shall find"?

HANNAH

I did, my son.
That you have sought, I know: that you have
found,
I will believe. But if a healthy tree,
Grafted with apple, bearing apple-flowers,
Should after yield a fruit we never saw,
What man would taste until he knew it safe?
Thus from the hope I nursed springs all at once
A something strange, sheer wonderment to me
That gave your nature most. How can I say

"Go on!" not knowing whither, or, "Come
back!"
Haply from good?

RHODA

Say nothing, then, but wait:
The way is fixed. I know not how I feel
His purpose; yet I feel, and follow him.

DAVID

Caught out of darkness, shall I turn my back
Against the light? or, spent from wildering ways,
Refuse the path that makes my feet secure?
I did not seek my struggle: it was there.
Why, men whose souls but burrow in their flesh
To feed, like worms in apples early ripe,
May say to mine: Be fat, and be content!
But me God sent the butterfly instead;
And it must flutter in the sun, or die.

PETER

(*Entering.*)

A stranger stands outside. He's one of them,
It seems, that you, that they— But come yourself:
Ten steps are easier than my telling it.

DAVID

What will he?

PETER

Preaching. There, the word is out!
You'll guess the rest.

[*Exit* DAVID.

ELKANAH

The business just goes on
As I expected! When was notion bred
By mortal brain, that did not set the tongue
In gear, to run full-tilt? He'll cackle, too,

So long as folks find something in his egg;
Then, maybe, when the thing's no longer fresh,
There'll be an end. He sows religious oats
A little heavier in the head, that's all;
But thorns and stony ground will waste the crop,
Or Gospel words mean nothing.

PETER

(*Aside to* RHODA.)

All the talk
(So this man says) in our and other towns
Is nought but David: there's no end of tales.
The moral of it they don't rightly know,
And bend their ear-flaps, like a restless horse,
To catch some new particular. If, now,
He has the call to preach, they have to hear.
'Twill come to that.

[*Exit.*

HANNAH

I never thought of you
As of a daughter, Rhoda; yet I see
That in your heart his ways are justified,
As in his own yourself. Men love the will
That bends to theirs; and she who fain would guide
Must seem to follow. I've directed him
Too long to make a new, obsequious change:
The place is yours. But, O my daughter (hence
I'll call you so), remember, never man,
Though gifted, raised, and made a power in the world,
Sufficed unto himself! Else he were god;
And she, the nearest, first, interpreting
All womankind to him, he, men to her,
Is called, as well, to claim her half of truth,
So testing his. I may have borrowed care
Where it was not intended: all that's come

Is what my natural sight had long foreseen,
Were it not partial. I must needs unloose
The precious bond of guidance, let him go,
And pray far-off, where once I held him close,
And breathed my heart in his believing ear.

RHODA

Grapes cannot come from thorns, but neither thorns
From fruitful vines. It is his blossom-time,
When storm or sudden chill may stint the fruit:
He should be sheltered. But my speech is scant;
And what I say sounds other than I feel.
So new the life is which he brings to mine,
So strange, exalted, I forget myself;
And, when he needs another's tongue, I fail.
You love him, you will shortly understand.
I will not take an atom that was yours
In all his thought: what he bestows on me
Is only love ungranted otherwise.

Scene VIII.

The same as Scene V. Some of the thickets on both sides of the brook have been roughly cleared away. A number of country-people, chiefly men, are gathered in the space thus made, — some seated on scattered stones, and stumps of trees; others approaching by the foot-path from below. Strong sunshine and heavy shadow alternately; an uncertain sky, portending storm.

FIRST MAN

'Tis a fool's errand that we come, I fear.

SECOND

He'll keep his word.

FIRST

Perhaps; but was it given?

THIRD

Ay, given to me. I offered him a chance
Open to use or let alone: he took

As eagerly as one that in the road
Sees a stray gold-piece.

SECOND

Be he cracked or sane,
Four days, they say, he fasted hereabouts,
Then, fresh and fair, went home. I'd not believe,
But for accounts of such and stranger things
Before our time.

FIRST

He's nowise different
From you or me. A little fresh conceit,
Like yeast, will puff a brain above its pan.

THIRD

It's more than that in him. He looked straight through
The face I had, and saw what lay below,—
Namely, no faith, but some curiosity,

A little fun withal; I hardly know, —
And smiled, but in a queer, forgiving way,
That hurt me afterwards.

SECOND

Stay, there he comes!
I mark no flighty or conceited airs, —
A plain young man, pale face, and shining eyes:
He mounts the rock. See how the sun comes out,
And strikes his head! Be silent, you! Sit down,
Make no disturbance, let him speak his mind!

DAVID

(*Standing upon the rock, sings:* RHODA *and* PETER, *below, join in the hymn.*)

Oh, praise the Lord the Giver!
  Relieve His burdened hands!
His miracles deliver
  The congregated lands:
He poureth as a river,
  And we but take the sands.

His fruitful boughs are shaken;
  His bounties fall as rain:
We sit with souls mistaken,
  In penitence and pain:
Awaken, world, awaken,
  And spread His feast again!

SECOND MAN

A gay beginning! I could join in that
With all my voice.

FIRST

They sing to lively tunes
In many churches.

THIRD

Yes, but say, the while,
They're stolen from the Devil. May be so;
But then the Devil must be a jolly soul,
And angels doleful as *Begone, dull care!*

DAVID

What come ye out to see? A reed in the wind?
But if God's lips unto a reed be set, —
The dryest one that whistles in the marsh, —
There comes a music that can soothe the world.
I make no claim: I tried to understand
The many promises that rust unused;
And all I asked, was, Are they granted yet?
Then, rising high as agony of prayer
May lift a mortal, lo! the answer came.
Show me the term, or limit! There is none:
Restore conditions, you restore the power;
And He who waiteth for a thousand years
Will manifest His wonders. They who teach,
You say, are silent as to this? Why, then
Let them make answer! Gifts of many tongues,

Of healing, miracle, and prophecy,
Given to His followers, by them to theirs,
Are buried treasures for this drowsy race.
He offering helmet, buckler, sword, and spear, —
Armor of proof, — perchance a shepherd's staff
We take, reluctant, mendicants where He
Awaits the guests that know their welcome sure.
So dust and cobwebs fill the temple; so
The cedarn beams are rotted in their place;
The trumps and timbrels crack, and wake no more
The songs of Zion: all is desolate,
As we were Israel that turned away!
'Tis time a mighty wind should whirl the chaff
From idle threshing-floors: my breath is weak,

So others not increase it, yet thou, Lord,
Who knowest whether I deserve or no
Thy signs of power, — who, should I point, as now,
My finger at the crest of yonder rock,
And say, "Be thou removed!" —

[*A part of the rock crashes down with a great noise and reverberation. Cries of terror, and much confusion among the people.*]

VOICES

It falls; it falls!
The world is coming to an end! He spake,
And it obeyed! A prophet, yea, a prophet!

DAVID

(*Who has remained quietly standing upon the rock, pale and rapt.*)

Be not afraid! The power that works within,
If it but shiver down one crumbling edge
Of old indifference, is mightier yet.
Therefore, I take it from His open hand,
Who made yon stones to fall. I hurl on you
His arrows, and the shining of His spear:
I bid believe, not me, but what, renewed,
In me is manifest: I call you back
From pools made muddy by the paddling feet
Of darkened generations, to the fount
He cleft, now gushing in a desert land.
He waits, how long! His summons, day by day —

[*Thunder and lightning.*]

VOICES

We do believe you. Turn His wrath away!
A Prophet, yea, a Prophet!

DAVID

There He spake:
Doubt not, as oft of old, but now attend
The voice within you, which is He indeed.
Oh! spread Thy banners on the streaming wind;
Come as the morning; broaden as the day;
Fill the dark places with Thy healing light;
And, once Thy reign assured, cast me aside,
So glorified in mine unworthiness,
Because I saw when Thou didst touch mine eyes!
Come, now, in thunder and the clouds of heaven,

And purifying cisterns of the rain,
To wash Thy world, and fit it for the sun!
Thy day is near at hand: the glory shed
With all Thy promises shall doubled be
On all Thy gifts.

[*A storm arises,—thunder, wind, and rain.*]

VOICES

A Prophet, yea, a Prophet!

ACT II.

SCENE I.

Afternoon. The crest of a rise, or swell, in a broad prairie. To the westward, in the distance, a line of timber, denoting the course of a stream; a train of emigrant-wagons scattered along the road thither. On the crest a solitary wagon, its canvas cover partly folded back. DAVID *and* RHODA, *with a child in her lap, seated in it;* PETER *standing at the horses' heads.*

RHODA

YOU'RE weary, husband: is it far to camp?

DAVID

Two hours, — to yonder smoky line of trees.
The signs of heaven are fair: the earth believes
In them, and, glad as any living thing,

Smiles far and wide. The sky is larger here,
And brighter; other life is in the winds;
The grass is lost beneath a waste of flowers:
It is our promised land.

RHODA

At last!

DAVID

Ah, me!

This weight and perilous sinking of the heart,
That ever looks before, or stubbornly
Tastes the o'ercome distresses of the past!
I gave the guidance of my mind away,
To be uplifted: now, on lower things,—
On trial, parting, woe of ignorant love,—
I dwell, as were they shadows coming on.

PETER

(*Sings.*)

We are swallows seeking the land of spring:
We are faint, we have far to roam:

When shall we fold the weary wing,
Lord, in Thy promised home?
Home!
We are bound for the promised home!

DAVID

How is it that I still upbear their souls?
The land, the temple, and His coming reign,
Through me, and their acceptance of my power,
Fill and content them: I should be content,
If human memories were not obstinate
As human needs. Do you remember still
The day that tried me most, and mother's words, —
"I cannot follow you, and dare not hold
Farewell! we shall not meet on earth again"?
What I obeyed expunged the seeming wrong,
But not its lingering sense; for while the wind
Blows softly over these unpeopled plains,
And in the middle watches of the night,
And when the young birds cheep their wish for morn,

I hear her say, and see her tearless eyes, —
"I cannot follow you, and dare not hold:
Farewell! we shall not meet on earth again."

RHODA

(*Bending over her child.*)

Sleep, baby, sleep! The wind will blow the flowers,
The trees will drop their berries, all for thee.

PETER

(*Sings.*)

We will build the temple broad and high,
And crowned with a golden dome;
For the day of the Lord is surely nigh,
When we reach the promised home.
Home!
We shall dwell in the promised home!

DAVID

They shame me, who have also left their all,
Save, nurtured with an easier hope, they bear

A lighter sorrow; yet as day by day
Their hosts increase, so mounts the sum of faith.
There was a woman came, a week agone,
To hear my message: on the outer edge
Of those few gathered in the dusky hall
She sat, and fixed me with her wondrous eyes.
At first I said, 'Tis Mary Magdalen,
Whose sin forgiven still left her virtue sad;
But, kindled with my words, the while I drew
A picture of the kingdom she became
Queen Esther, as in Shushan's royal house
She touched the sceptre, proud, obedient,
Sure of the end. A power came forth from her,
As if of wings companioning mine own.
Can she believe, nor follow?

RHODA

Rather think
On these your faithful flock. If she have power,

Indeed, the greater sin of pride is hers,
Whose gold and gay apparel are her gods.

DAVID

(*Musingly.*)

The light of guidance never was so clear
And then deceived: what instruments I have —
Rough hands of workmen, by whose awkward use
The gifts almost become a mockery —
Still leave me helpless when the finer sense
Would snatch from floating lines a plan supreme.
There must be law, pure discipline of lives,
Foundations set, and pleasant sheepfolds made
In desolate places. Ah! were only one
But near me, bathed in equal bliss of faith,
To see, where I am dazzled, and to say,
"Build higher! here enlarge the pillared front,
There push thy climbing pinnacles aloft!"
Even light is lonely to a human soul.

Two glories are there; and but one they know,
Save her who saw, then closed reluctant eyes.

RHODA

Can you be faint of spirit while by you
We all are led? Then is the body weak,
And rest will be your medicine.

DAVID

(*To* PETER)

Go on!

PETER

(*Driving onward, sings.*)

The bolts of the Lord shall fall and burn
  On Babylon and on Rome;
But the chosen seed shall safe return,
  To dwell in His promised home.
                Home!
  We have found His promised home!

Scene II.

Night. A camp on the banks of a small stream. Men, women, and children grouped about fires under the trees. In the centre a tent, before which a pole, stuck in the earth, bears a blazing torch. Outside of the camp a guard is heard to challenge some one approaching. After the pass-word, "Zion," enter Nimrod Kraft. *He dismounts from his horse, and draws near the tent.*

NIMROD

Hail, Prophet David! Grace and blessing be
To all the chosen!

DAVID

Be the words fulfilled!
You come beforehand, like the dove, to say
The waters settle, and the olive-tree
Puts forth new leaves. We shall possess the land.

NIMROD

We *do* possess it. On the highest bluff
That overlooks full twenty miles of stream,

Now stand a hundred cabins: we have staked
The streets, first measured with the holy reed,
And broken cornfields from the stubborn sod,
And set young gardens round about the place,
That much do flourish. Every work is blessed:
Even the quarry-stones come loose in squares,
As if they hastened to be lifted up,
And made the temple.

DAVID

Ah! when once it stands,
A visible sign, a shelter for our ark!

NIMROD

Even so we feel. They give their tithing-time
In faith and in rejoicing; I have used
The power you delegated to my hands,
Sifted the wheat, and sent some chaff adrift,
Fixed ordered rule, exacted industry,

And so blocked roughly out what you may shape
To pure proportions: as my work below
Grows up, may yours complete it from above!

DAVID

Let all the frame-work needful for our flock,
As shelter, or enclosing law, be raised,
And quickly. I have given you the Twelve;
Yet they debate, methinks, or seek to know
Who shall sit highest.

NIMROD

Thus it was of old.
Your headship must remain; for you alone
Possess direct commission. Let them see —
They whom your messengers found here and there,
And, not beholding, none the less believe —
What power is yours. A little thing's enough.

DAVID

What mean you?

NIMROD

Well, I find it natural.
Your coming will be made a holy day;
For all shall then be gathered as a brood
Beneath your wings. And something they expect,
Some sign, or show, as reconfirming faith;
Or revelation, such as ignorant souls
Gape at and glory in. None promised this:
But they believe; and therefore they expect.

DAVID

When I was small, I planted once a tree,
Then every second morning plucked it up
To see if it were growing. Summer came;
And while the others, left alone, were green,
Mine pined and perished. Give the flock, instead,
This parable.

NIMROD

They would not understand.
Transplanted faith (let me the rather say)
Needs watering, shelter, all the gardener's care,
Till it be rooted. Ponder this yourself.
Put on your sandals; leave the holier ground,
And walk in dust among the multitude:
So shall you feel their need.

DAVID

I never asked
But what is offered freely unto all.
There is no flame, it seems, that of itself
Will burn in earthly air; but, then, is flame,
When fed from coarser aliment, less pure?
Water pollutes itself from what is washed;
But fire takes up its own, and spurns the dross.
If that were possible to me —

NIMROD

Yourself
Shall winnow, with a finer fan than ours,
Whom we have gathered. All is ready, else.
I will not keep your body from its rest.
With Hugh and Jonas, members of the Twelve,
I must consult, so portioning the homes,
That none shall mark advantage of the rest.
The flock is jealous: softly on the nose
Must we pat every sheep, as well as feed.

[*Exit.*

DAVID

(*To* RHODA, *who has overheard the dialogue.*)

There goes a sense with which I cannot strive,
So well it builds, and so obediently;
Yet power is lessened when it touches me.

RHODA

I did not like the man, when he — I mean
His hardness first repelled; but now, perhaps,

He is the coarser fuel, you the flame;
And each may need the other. I, too, feel
That they which follow, never having seen,
Deserve a sign.

DAVID

If so, the Lord will send.
[*Exit into the tent.*

RHODA

Not their belief, but who it is believes,
Gives him support. That was a happy time,
When we alone went wandering through the land;
For few could jeer, though many sore abused;
And ever here and there a soul was caught
Out from the Gentiles, and was glad with us;
And Zion with its temple shone afar,
More beautiful, I think, than now at hand.
I must not murmur: we are verily blessed,

Put past the reach of persecuting hands,
And guided so, that this fair wilderness
Already bears the roses as we pass.

Scene III.

Another part of the camp. Nimrod, Hugh, *and* Jonas *seated near a fire.*

HUGH

He will not, think you?

NIMROD

Nay, I said not that.
I only charge that nothing be proclaimed;
Then whatsoever come, if so it come,
Will have more operation. See, the flock
Is over-hungry for continual signs;
Which, could they be bespoken, would be nought
But independence of the Lord.

JONAS

Maybe.
But I that chose the gift of healing, I
That have obeyed in all things, I should heal!
If he must husband up his power to spend
On higher miracles, enough is mine
For lesser work: so strengthen, then, my hands,
That they on whom I lay them shall be whole.

NIMROD

The wish may choose: possession comes by faith.
Know surely that you have it, and you have.

JONAS

How know without a test?

NIMROD

Ah! there you lack
The last anointing; there the prophet stands
Transparent in his own internal light,

While yours is cloudy still. When you foresee
The healing of your hands, your hands will heal.

HUGH

So works the gift? But, if *his* foresight be
Indeed so perfect, it were rude to say,
As cheer to some, and guidance unto all,
This member strays, that rises; these receive,
Or lose, that our authority be firm;
For such picked out for higher reach of faith
Will stand, supporting us, above the rest.

NIMROD

First show them patience! Gathered here and
there,
The dust of other life upon their shoes,
The stagnant blood of other creeds not yet
Purged from their veins, the Gentile taunt still
loud
In ear and memory, restless from the change

And long privation of the pilgrimage,
They hear but halfly: we must give them rest,
Fitting their shoulders to an easy yoke,
Filling their cribs, and warmly bedding them,
Till they will rather serve within our fold
Than rule outside of it.

JONAS

Is all prepared
For us who come? The people hear of those
Who, first arriving, may be better placed.

NIMROD

I did not take my gift of prophecy
In vain: so ye declare it unto all,
Contentment waits for woman, man, and child;
But to yourselves I promise more belief.
Go, hither bring the tally of your men:
My work is yet unfinished.

[*Exit* HUGH *and* JONAS.]

All alike!

No one is certain that he has the power,
Unless his neighbor says so. Tell them, then,
They govern, governing myself the while.
So far were easy: yet from him comes forth
The fire that makes their dull cold metal bend;
And when to kindle it is in his will,
Not mine. He has a look of weariness;
And out of languor comes no miracle.
But oft, from very expectation, springs
The thing expected, if a cooler skill
Command the heat of others. What she plans —
If any thing, indeed — I cannot guess;
Not even whether like or dislike looked
From eyes that only seemed to hide her thought.
Turn either way, I'm poking in the dark.
Well, well! the morrow is the clearer day.

Scene IV. — The City.

A street on a high, airy plateau, overlooking the course of a great river. In the centre stand the unfinished walls of the temple; opposite to them a house larger than the others, its front hung with garlands, and an arch of green boughs spanning the entrance. The people, several hundred in number, are drawn up in lines on both sides of the street, with branches in their hands. Shouts are heard in the distance, announcing the arrival of the train: then David *appears on horseback, a little in advance, bare-headed, and wearing a long white mantle: the people cast their branches before him.*

HYMN.

We have left the land of Egypt
  For the place of our desire:
Fallen is the gated city;
  And the woe thereof is dire:
The boughs of the tree are withered,
  And the women set them on fire!

Lo! who is he that cometh
  In the name of the Holy One?
The bearers of gladsome tidings
  Before his pathway run:
He bringeth us out of darkness,
  As the star that brings the sun.

[*The women step forward on each side, and sing,* LIVIA ROMNEY, *with a crown in her hand, standing in the midst.*]

Hail, all hail, to the prophet,
  Whose reign begins to-day!
Who hath laid his firm foundations
  In the dust of the world's decay:
He maketh the dry bough blossom;
  He gathers the sheep that stray.

DAVID

(*Aside.*)

It is herself! How beautiful she stands,
Forgetful of the stare of wondering eyes,
And filled with promise of mysterious power!
She's Miriam now, and sings deliverance.

I breathe again: the weight falls off my soul,
As poising rocks are started by a sound;
And I am glad and strong for what may come.

LIVIA

(*Stepping forward.*)

Thrice hail, O Prophet! Bow but once before
Thy humble handmaid, not as honoring her,
But that she reach thy consecrated brow.

[*David bends down his head: she places the crown upon it.*]

Forgive me, that, when first I did believe,
I failed to follow: thus it came to pass
I went before to seal mine evidence,
Lest that were vain which I would ask of thee.

HUGH

(*To* NIMROD.)

Who is the woman?

NIMROD

More than is her name
I cannot say. 'Tis but four days ago
She landed from the river. Worldly store
She seems to have, and knowledge of the world,
Notable cunning of the hand and eye,
And influence with her sex — perhaps with ours.
Foremost in planning this array was she;
Went here and there; was always first and last;
And therefore fell to her, by proper right,
The place she wanted.

DAVID

(After a pause.)

Thou art one of us.
There is no high or low: each bows to each
In whom the Spirit lives. I saw thy faith,
And called thee: well it was that thou didst hear.
Not they who yield when buffeted by words,

And shaken by the signs, but they who feel,
Like wandering birds, where lies the summer-land,
And strike their way across the printless air,
Build up the kingdom. Thine obedience
Is as a soil for planting of the power.
What is it thou wouldst ask?

LIVIA

The gift of tongues.

DAVID

(*After looking in her face a moment, beckons. She comes nearer.*)

Take thou the gift, in measure as thy faith
Shall justify, and even so exercise.

LIVIA

(*Steps back a pace, keeping her eyes fixed on* DAVID. *She rises to her full height, with uplifted head, and points towards the temple.*)

Aïro pamétha loydór óndis abárka!

[*Movements and murmurs among the people.*]

A MAN

What tongue is that?

A SECOND

It must be ancient Greek,
Or Hebrew, maybe, as Isaiah spoke.
The sound is glorious.

A THIRD

Never did I hear
Such mighty words. Our preacher once came down
With "Armageddon, Pandemonium, Baal;"
But they were nought to hers.

THE FIRST.

'Tis prophecy!
He understands: his face is like a flame.

LIVIA

Oráthmedón ádra, bánnorim ádra slávo!

DAVID

(*Rapidly and eagerly.*)

It *shall* arise! The tempests of the world
Shall not prevail against it! Every stone
Shall testify! From its completed towers
A light go forth till darkened Edom sees;
And here, even here, where our Shechinah stands,
When all mankind is gathered to our fold,
Shall angels plant the ladder of the Lord
For His descending. Be ye not as them
That craved new signs, and were rebuked of Him!
Who feeleth not the presence of the power
Above us, in us, moving in our works,
And only sparing insomuch as saves
From easy heart, slack will, and idle hand,
Let him go forth!

CRIES OF THE PEOPLE

Nay, nay, we will abide!

DAVID

Forget that you have ever lived ere now.
As strips the serpent her uneasy skin,
And comes forth new and shining, cast ye out
Old hopes and hates, old passions and desires.
Be as a fallow field that waits new seed:
Take rain and sunshine in their times; lie bare
To the invisible influence of heaven;
And be assured from your warm breast shall spring
The holy harvest! Ye have welcomed me
With faithful hearts and voices: so, henceforth
No more as one that in the wilderness
Cries to the stocks and stones, shall I be heard,
But as a father 'mid his children teach,
And as a brother 'mid his brethren love,
And as one chosen lead ye all to share
An equal power and glory.

THE PEOPLE

Hail, all hail!

NIMROD

(*Coming forward.*)

Here is your home: by her on whom the tongue
Descended at your bidding, it was dressed.
The humble house is like a bride that waits
The bridegroom's coming: enter, and be blessed!
I, and my brethren of the Twelve, have charge
That all, ere nightfall, shall be snugly housed,
New brethren mixed with old, but in such peace
And kindly fellowship, as, until now,
Hath not been witnessed, to the world's disgrace!

THE WOMEN

(*At a sign from* LIVIA, *sing.*)

Make haste, Belovèd of Zion!
The porch and the chamber shine:
We have gathered the myrrh and manna,
And filled the flagons with wine:
Now comfort the souls of thy daughters,
As the Lord shall comfort thine.

[DAVID *waits, standing under the arch, while* PETER *assists* RHODA *to alight from the wagon.*]

PETER

Well, here's the end! Our Zion's rather bare,
But makes a good beginning.

RHODA

(*Giving him her child.*)

Carry him,
But hold him gently: he is tired and scared.
I, too, am wearier than I thought to be,
And hardly happy in beholding home
Till I possess it. David, come with me!

[*They enter the house.*

Scene V.

The council-room. Night. Nimrod Kraft, Hugh, Jonas, Simeon, *and two other members of the Twelve.*

NIMROD

All now are housed and sleeping: first their souls

Were satisfied, and then their bodies soothed.
On this rock must we build. The arch of truth
Requires abutments in the life of flesh:
It cannot hang in air. See, therefore, ye,
That these the weak foundations of our state
Be firmer settled. Scourge the drones away;
Over the labor needful unto each
Be labor added for the sake of all.
Let him whose lips are not anoint believe
With hand and sinew!

JONAS

If the hand should doubt?
Equality of service and of power
Was promised them; and many bear the yoke
As they that seem to stoop, and mean to spring.

NIMROD

Equality? Yes, were there equal faith.
Not yet dare I to measure mine by his,
The Prophet's, since the token lies in power.
They sleep; we watch for them: why, let them
  watch,
And we will sleep.

SIMEON

Then wolves would rend the fold.
The new life must begin: he spake the word.
It will be hard; but we submit to him,
And they not more so, in obeying us.

JONAS

How far will he concede? The government,
Scarce framed as yet, will he alone direct,
Uncounselled, or be led to side with them
Who, standing nearest, easier prevail?
Whence comes decision, when opinions clash?

NIMROD

By revelation.

SIMEON

May it come at need!

HUGH.

We, the apostles of the wandering church,
Should be, of right, foundations here.

NIMROD

He takes,
Lifts up, or sets aside. You know my work,
If it be good. I never thought to say,
"Reward me!" but whatever implement, —
Scythe-blade, or sword, or knife that scullions use, —
His hand has need of, he will find me that!

JONAS

(*Aside to* HUGH.)

When one is sword already, sharpened too,
The offer's glibly made.

NIMROD

I say but this:
It was my providence to know him first,
To see descending on him, like a flame,
The Spirit: near, because alone, I stood,
But am less near than he who more believes.
What use of prying words? 'Tis signs we need,
Accord of all. The temple-walls complete
With roof and pinnacle, the shrine set up,
Symbolic vessels, altar, veil, and ark,
New psalms of praise, and joyfulness of hymns,—
All this made visible. Their faith is firm;
And their impatient thoughts, now floating loose
In every wind, will settle, and have rest.

[*Exit* HUGH, JONAS, *and others.*

SIMEON

You touched his secret sore,—I name no names,—
Kept tender, as I guess, by discontent
Of womankind. You've seen the kind of wife
That never wholly justifies the man,
And, when he follows, straightway shifts her mind
To make new disagreement: such is she.
With brethren one must be considerate,
As you have been; but those whom now he makes
Apostles should not wear a home-made bit.
That I am widowed, nigh a blessing seems,
Though mine respected me.

NIMROD

The words I spake
Were but the Prophet's unpronounced desires.
I am the nearest yet, because I keep

A circle round him clear and unprofaned,
That so his soul be tempered to receive
Continual revelations. They mistake
Probation, preparation, for the end.
But that which draws the few is not enough
To sow infection in the blood of all,
And overcome the world. Much more awaits,
And grander: are you as the fallow earth?

SIMEON

Yea, passive as a field the sower treads.

NIMROD

'Tis well: till he shall order otherwise,
Be led by me! Go, now, and counterwork
The small dissensions: I have other tasks.
It was a wondrous sign that heralded
The Prophet's coming: keep the wonder fresh
In all, yet raise not wild and over-wrought
Expectancy of more. The woman's power

Renews another ancient virtue lost, —
Zion shall have its prophetess! I go
To give my homage, and to arm for us
A Deborah, — a chieftainess of the faith.

Scene VI.

A room in the Prophet's *house.* Rhoda *seated near the window, sewing; the baby asleep in a cradle at her feet;* David *at a desk, looking over some papers.*

DAVID

The man must have commission from the Lord,
To plan such perfect system: not the bees
Get wax and honey, build their brittle combs,
And organize their kingdom of the hive,
So faultlessly. My loss of power through him
Was but a fancy bred of weariness;
For what he asked of my unwilling soul
Came, half a marvel to myself.

RHODA

I, too,
Have thought him hard: he lacked your sweeter fire.
Yet surely something kindly planned this home,
Not chance, to give the dear familiar rooms
We first were happy in. Young trees are set,
Like children of the old ones following us,
In the same places, by the southern porch;
And in the garden — foolishly I cried
To find the cushions of the mountain-pink
And yellow-flags, and fragrant southern-wood.
Can this again be taken? Will there come
Aught to disturb us?

DAVID

Nay, it cannot be.
We build too surely: we are set alone
In a new land. Why should the Gentiles mock

The boasted precedent whereon they build,
Their right of conscience, by molesting us?

(*Enter* PETER.)

PETER

The town is ringing with the miracle.
Whether 'twas Hebrew, or the sort of tongue
That Adam spoke, they're not exactly sure;
But 'twas a prophecy, and will fulfil.
Then, since it seems there's here and there a man
Talks Dutch, or French, or maybe Cherokee, —
They're all as one to them that never learned, —
She understood 'em! 'Twas a coming down
Of tongues, they say, just like what happened once
Away in Mesopotamia.

DAVID

Given at need!
By this I know the woman's lofty faith,

And eminence of prayer. Why, save myself,
Not one hath been so visited. New flames
Circling mine own, kindled in souls like hers,
Will help fend off the slow, devouring chill
That from the fiend is blown.

RHODA

I thought her strange,
Scarce one of us, so grand and beautiful
And unabashed. I should be grateful, though,
She drew away so many eyes that else
Had stared in wonder I should be your wife.

PETER

They say, in getting up the welcome-home,
And such pontificals, she steered the raft.
Willing or not, or knowing things or not,
All, somehow, lent a hand: she had a way
To make them satisfied with what they did.

Talk of the — well, it nearly slipped that time —
Of *her*, and she appears.

[*Exit.*

RHODA

(*Aside.*)

I cannot stir,
Lest baby wake; and sure my place is here;
Yet would that she were come and gone again!

[LIVIA *enters: she is simply but elegantly dressed in a black silk robe, and wears a white veil upon her head.*]

DAVID

(*Taking her hand.*)

Be welcome, sister! If I thank you less
For honor paid than for unstinted faith,
I most am grateful.

LIVIA

What I fain had said
Falls back upon my heart as hollow sound.

Your soul hath read, and, reading, spares me
words
That only stammer when my own would sing.
The marvellous light that entered me from you
I cannot fathom, nay, nor merit it,
Except in yielding, in receiving all,
As woman may, in whom the sense is quick
To conquer reason which resists in man.
I was a harp-string, mute until you touched:
If to your ear the sound be melody,
Strike out of me the strong, full-handed chords
To your exaltment.

DAVID

(*Aside, as* LIVIA *goes forward to* RHODA.)

When was ever such?
The clear-eyed spirit, so superbly housed,
The power that bends in soft subservience,
The gift that beams on all except herself, —

Yea, she is chosen. Yea, from out her eyes,
And from her hands, and breathing forth from
her,
Is promise.

LIVIA

(*To* RHODA.)

You, whose blessed place it is
To touch and warm the Prophet's weary hands,
And, after shining visions, to restore
The virtue of his dazzled eyes, be kind,
I pray, and friendly! I would have *your* love,
His confidence. My life was not as yours,
Ah, me! as simply innocent and pure;
And yet, methinks, for them that meet in truth,
There's but a single gateway to the heart.

RHODA

(*Slowly.*)

I think I never hated such as seemed

Unfriendly: if I fail to love, when love
Invites me first, I were not worthy it.

LIVIA

(*Turning to* DAVID.)

My lines of life, as they draw near to you,
Lie clearly traced; yet, as they backward tend,
Lead to confusions which, ere knowing them,
Your pardon touched. The spoiled child of the
world
Was I until I saw you; born in wealth,
And cradled 'mid the shows and vanities
Religion covers with a modish cloak.
Pride to the right, to left stood Piety:
Each took a hand, and grimly led my life
Along the pavement trod by feet of all.
When I would wander free, as whoso feels
Some independent right of soul, gave Pride
A downright blow that stung; but Piety

Pinched me in secret, while her leaky eyes
Wept rivers, and her whining voice bewailed.
Then I submitted, lived a ceaseless lie,
Till death and changes had delivered me
From all but wealth. But, ah! my fettered limbs
Were dwarfed and shrunken: I was free to move,
When motion was but pain. I saw the world
As one beholds a casket, and the key
Thereof is lost. I stood outside of life,
Helpless to reach existence I desired,
Disgusted with existence which I knew,
Until you said, or through your soul I heard,
"Daughter, arise!" and I arose and came.

DAVID

Not I, but what in me was manifest.

LIVIA

It is the same. By you alone I heard,
Through you am satisfied. I hardly knew

What gift to claim, till something in your face
Gave me the words. But now, farewell! I go
To cheer, perchance to help, the others.

[*Exit.*

DAVID

Go!
Delivered, thou, and crowned! A woman's hand
I had forgotten: yet it saved of old,
And here may build, as well.

RHODA

Your lamp is lit
You know whereat; and theirs are lit from yours.

DAVID

Fire hath one being: 'tis the life that makes
Obscure or luminous; and hers, suppressed
By darkening hands, breaks out in splendid blaze.
She waited for me: I have bid her shine.

ACT III.

Scene I.

A room in the Prophet's *house.* David, Nimrod, *and* Livia *seated at a table upon which lie papers and plans.* Rhoda *at the window looking upon the garden, with some needlework in her hand.*

NIMROD

It means not failure. Still our armor shines,
Our weapons cleave; but they whose power we shake,
The lazy priesthood of neglected law,
Have clothed themselves with cunning, to evade
Direct assault: so on their flanks exposed
Must we surprise them.

DAVID

Yet I would not haste.
Even after goodly battle, here we sit
Not quite secure; for jealousy of some,
Unreasoning hopes that in denial end,
And selfish fretting o'er each needful curb,
Still task our wisdom: hardly can we spare
The fine, selected strength your purpose claims.

NIMROD

There is no virtue but fatigues itself.
A sudden truth uplifts with violence
The prostrate human soul; but once exhaust
The first impulsion, see how weak it stands!
So there's a crisis this side of success
In highest things: our lot, this hour, is weighed
With that of all neglected, powerless tribes,
That have no life but in the founder's name.
If here we pause, we may become as they;

But if, accepting every sign of power
As loan, or test, until another come,
We lime new branches, and extend our nets
To snare men's fluttering souls, we shall possess,
In time, the world.

LIVIA

Surely no less will you,
Our prophet; and no atom less will we.
That few are gathered now, and halting minds
Grow restless, casts no shadow on the truth;
For souls are verily but as frightened birds
That beat themselves against the pane, and shun
The hand that catches them to set them free.

NIMROD

Well spoken! Nothing more have I proposed.

DAVID

I hoped direct, immediate influence —
The power that kindles, burns, and purifies —

Might be all-potent: yet, if men avoid
The touch of healing, must be first constrained,
Till health and gratitude together work
To bring them here, I cannot but receive.

NIMROD

Then, if they come, why question how they come?
The life delivered never faulty finds
The manner of deliverance. I, once,
When caught by drowning arms that would have
drowned
Me also, dealt a powerful blow that stunned
And saved the man.

LIVIA

Deal out your blows to men,
And welcome! Women claim a gentler touch.
How many are there, discontented hearts
That pine and wither, seeking sympathy

Their sex denies, and yours in half-contempt
Neglects to give! For virile souls are coarse
And awkward, being selfish: the plain way
To woman's fast dependence (which she thinks
Dependence on her) you would seek in vain,
Unless an Ariadne gave the clew.

NIMROD

Who, then, was she? A Gentile woman, sure,
Whom Paul converted.

LIVIA

'Tis enough that she
Was woman, and enough that also I
Am woman. Once I dwelt in Rome, it chanced;
And thither came a spinster whom I knew,
Free of the world, indifferent to love,
Secure and calm in high intelligence,
Armed at all points; yet soon the Church espied
Beneath cold breasts the vulnerable sense.

The haughty priests, whose passionless, thin lips
So rarely, but with dangerous sweetness, smile,
The dreamy youths, the rosy acolytes,
Sang to her, gave their faith the form of love,
Till with new passion, as in budding years,
Her woman's heart, sore with long abstinence,
Sent up narcotic heats that drugged the brain,
And she was theirs. As easily were she ours!
There is no woman lives but in her soul
Demands a bridegroom; failing one of flesh,
Then one of spirit. Learn to promise this
In secret visitations, mystic signs,
Make truth seem love, and knowledge ecstasy,
And you will lead our sex.

RHODA

(*Rising hastily.*)

Who, then, are *you?*
What mother nursed you on such milk as this?

I have but scanty words; but in my heart
The woman, from her simple whiteness torn,
And dipped in scarlet, cries, "Not thus are we!
Not thus the loneliness of maiden life,
The lingering sorrow of frustrated love,
And pure regret, and tender hope outlived,
Seek compensation." Less than moveth man
Gives woman peace. The aged, innocent lives
Of childless widows and unwedded maids
Softly enclose us, young, and keep from harm.
Denied their own, they guard another's brood,
So gathering bliss. But of what kind are those
Who find no truth, save men, forbid to wed,
Or wived already, offer it as love?

LIVIA

Your innocence takes false alarm: the old,
The gentle, fixed in narrow circumstance,
Good by tradition and temptation's lack,

Resist us most. Who was it came to call
Not righteous men, but sinners? Virtue lifts
A front the braver after knowledge comes;
But is not knowledge first? I spake of that
Whereof your ignorance is no reproach:
The blessedness of life descends on you,
But not on them you blame.

DAVID

Reject not such!
'Twas so commanded: them the Devil traps
It may be lawful that we snare in turn.
We fight the Fiend, my wife: our triumph here
Hath pricked him out of ancient confidence.

NIMROD

The power is given: the secret of its use
Is left to us. The first light dazzles men;
And some reach forth, and grasp the guiding hand;

Then others say, with pupils narrowed in,
"There is no need: we see but as we saw."
Here, husbanding the busy strength of all,
And wasting nought, the comforts we can spare
Invite a double number: let them come!
And if, through weakness captured, they receive
The gift of power; through greed, unselfishness;
Through vain delusions, knowledge of the truth, —
What fool will cast away the tested gold
He gets, for promised copper?

LIVIA

Strange that men
Who most do suffer must be driven to good!
They are as children bribed to take the draught
That saves, even though the prophet's honeyed
wine.
Lo! now the temple's gilded pinnacles
The impatient sun hath kissed: across the land

They sharply shine like arrows drawn to head,
And heavenward aimed. The signs portend
increase.
Shall we alone be lean, while others burst
With useless fatness?

DAVID

Call our messengers
To learn a new commandment! We must stay
Their sinking hands, fill up their flickering lamps,
And sting their souls with courage which o'er-
comes,
Since it foresees. One weapon given to all
Were scarcely wisdom: lend the shorter arm
A longer blade, the less-enduring force
Advantage of the ground. While they exist,
The Gentile churches, must we spread or cease.
I meant not idleness; but, if so seems
This pause of preparation, let us work

Amid the noises of the ringing steel,
Heat with quick hammer-blows where fire may fail,
And only rest when faint with victory.

Scene II.

The council-room. David *seated in an arm-chair at the head of a long table;* Nimrod *at the foot; on each side, six members of the* Council of Twelve.

DAVID

Not every leaf an equal bounty finds
Of sap or sun; yet rooted is our State
To grow, and not to wither. We must sweep
The troubled waters of the world, henceforth,
In wider circles, luring to our ark
Them, chiefly, for the covenant who yearn,
And would behold, distinct as graven words,
The signs thereof in us. If any here,
In view of such advantage, hath inquired,

And finds a partial answer in his soul,
Let him be heard!

NIMROD

Some brethren, with myself
(For scattered duties scarce allow, as yet,
Full conference), have found accordant minds.
We, least of all fore-grasping power reserved,
Put forth projecting lines of present power
To their conclusions in the future, reach
This argument: We dare not mutilate
Our restoration of neglected faith
By preaching only: it must live in us
Until the ancient days and ways He loved
Shall draw Him near, — not simply where the soul
Trims her small chamber, or prophetic lips
Burn from His fiery touch; but call Him down,
To make His very self endurable
To human sense. A trance, mistook for death,

Thaws from the blood with struggle and with pang;
And still we feebly move the torpid limbs,
See through a veil, and hear but muffled sounds:
So you, whose hand upon us broke the spell,
Give, pulse by pulse, the life revealed to you,
As we take strength to bear it.

JONAS

Not to me
Was this imparted, nor to some I know.
There may be times demanding cloudy speech;
But clearer now were welcomer. What pulse
Shall first be felt? The prophet called on us,
I thought; and you direct us back to him.

SIMEON

Without conferring, unprepared as you,
Yet do I comprehend. The cloud may be
Inside of eyes that blame the sky for it.

NIMROD

Nay, Simeon! He who speaks in images
Oft sees the image taken for the thing.
Hear, all! We mean to purchase power disused,
But never abrogated: on what rock,
If not on this, have we been building here?
And he who welds again the broken link
Between the Lord and man, who summon us
To twofold lives that speak our waxing faith, —
Ah! once let morning rise, men soon forget
Their hours of darkness, — he awaits that we
Obey his messages in soul and flesh.

HUGH

Then what is past is sealed, our work approved
And fresh apportioned?

DAVID

Is not all one piece, —
Past, present, future, — as a youth in whom

The child expands, the man is possible?
This restless ferment in the general mind
Must not infect my own: the charge ye bear
I gave, indeed; but, save by constant guard
And forceful lifting of the soul, I keep
The separate gift, then were ye lost with me.
What I anticipate I dare not speak,
Until commanded. Voices heard from far,
And shadows thrown, are stammering messengers;
But when His will, in language and in form,
Arrives, the time of conference is past.
Speak, now, and freely: therefore I withdraw.

[*Exit.*

HUGH

His words hold promise: he was highly moved.
Yet, if the revelation must forbid
All further question, why confer we now?

MORDECAI

In holy discipline. We, too, have felt
The breathing of the Spirit; and our souls
Point, like the smallest flame, the way it draws:
So, after him if now our light be cast,
We lead the others.

NIMROD

Yea: what I declared
Was but direction, not a single path.
Who our accomplished work in truth accepts
Will halt not here; but, bending yearning eyes
Upon their lives, who owned the heritage
From Dan and Hermon unto Hebron's oaks,
Will scan each custom, pleasant to the Lord,
And choose what fails us most. Let, therefore, each
Go back in spirit, serve in Jacob's stead;
Behold the sons of Aaron with strange fire

Consumed, and stoned the son of Shelomith;
Tarry with Judah where the way goes up
To Timnath; find his feet, like Boaz, warm
From her who stole beneath the garment's skirt;
Or, set in fruitful households, chant the psalms
Of shepherd-kings, and Solomon's high song.
All He allowed — nay, so encouraged, then,
He turned aside, and in the heat of day
Did visit His elected — must be ours,
Ere we, with hands and meats no more unclean,
Dare dress the board for Him. What first to choose
Of new adornment for the mighty Guest
Is now our task.

JONAS

You had not said so much,
Save you had chosen. Let us know your choice.

MORDECAI.

While we aspire, it seems you'd fain provoke
Dissension: rather to the records turn,
Dead histories so long, but now brought near
For pure example.

SIMEON

Why, what words are his?
From our beginning we have trod one track —

NIMROD

(*Interrupting.*)

Which leads straight forward, over cowardice,
And half-belief, and forms of later law
God never gave. What says the foolish world?
That place and time and circumstance have changed:
Still those were holy men. But what they did
Makes us unholy. Oh! He loved them well,

Stepped down from heaven upon their herded
    hills,
Talked face to face. So much priests bid us take,
Then — there they halt; and all emasculate law
They teach, casts dirt on Israel of old.
Of kings, or prophets, or apostles, none
Forbids our following: every sign bestowed
On our new eyes says, Conquer all by all!

SIMEON

(*Aside to Hugh.*)

He waxes mighty.

NIMROD

'Tis enough to-day!
The Prophet's words give guidance to our thoughts.
Let each into the closet of his soul
Retire a space, and there, alone, select
Not what the weakening leaven of the past,
And unabolished habit of the heart,

Stir up within us; but the thing he finds
Chiefest in ancient lives, and lacking here.
It may be we shall wander different ways;
But all lead forward, and will surely join.

Scene III.

A garden in the rear of the Prophet's *house.* Peter *digging a bed.*

PETER

(*Pausing in his work.*)

I hardly ought to say it; but you can't
Turn one thing into t'other. Leastways, some
Have only changed their devils, not cast out,
And, with the pick and choice of gifts they had,
Are none the wiser. There my old horse-sense
Said, just as plain, "See whether you can use;"
And, if I'd opened mouth, and shut my eyes,
The Lord knows whether any thing had dropped.

I can't make out: there's going back and forth,
Like candidates before election-time,
When, with a little sleight-of-hand, a man
May sell two votes. Here mine will hardly count.
Our David's always safe, and Brother Kraft,
And Sister Livia, — each a regiment.
She looked at me in such an asking way,
This morning! what the — Zion — could she want?
Maybe, the temple — more pontificals:
Whichever way you turn, when sundown comes,
It's temple, temple, temple! I was glad
On their account; but, now it's finished up,
Both him and her go sideling round the house,
As if forever hunting something lost.

[*Sings.*]

Oh! I've a hundred acres of land,
  And a house to cover your head;
And in the spring, when the dovey-doveys sing,
  They say it's the time to wed.

Oh! I've an eye that is blue and shy,
  And a mouth that is red, says she,
And a heart at rest in my lily, lily breast;
  And why should I wed with thee?

Oh! take your choice when the days are long,
  And be sure you never will rue.
When I'm safe from storm, and it's bonny, bonny warm,
  Say, what will become of you?

Oh! I'll comb and curl your bright brown hair,
  On a Sunday morning gay;
For a maid, I guess, when she means yes, yes,
  Begins with a nay, nay, nay!

NIMROD

(*Entering.*)

When birds sing that way, it is time to build.
Good-morrow, Peter!

PETER

And good-day, high priest!

[*Aside.*]

I have a vote, it seems.

NIMROD

Your plants are trim
And forward: that shows liking for the place.
The Prophet told me, as an orphan boy
You came to him.

PETER

Ay, 'twas my only home.

NIMROD

Your silent faith counts more than that of some
Who make a loud profession. Modestly
You choose no gift; but you may highly serve
The Church, by being fully what you are.

PETER

Preambles don't get through my head.

NIMROD

Find, then,
A mate, and add a dozen to our flock.

PETER

Oho! That's good advice. But here's my fix:
I stand half-way 'twixt Jane and Mary Ann
(We'll say), both willing. Now, to choose for good,
When, either took, you might find afterwards
The t'other was the better, — there *I* stick!
I'd let our Rhoda pick for me; but then,
She don't know both.

NIMROD

(Lowering his voice.)

If both were given to you,
As in the days of old?

PETER

(Dropping his spade.)

That's something new:
You mean it?

NIMROD

What has been may be again.

PETER

Well, each is pleasant while she holds the chance,
And would outbid the t'other: make it law
For all of us, the double check would last,
And they'd pull square, I guess.

NIMROD

What thus relieves
Your own dilemma offers general peace.
But guard your tongue: I've no authority
To promise this, or even so much as hint.
You've read your Bible: what the Lord himself
Established for the fathers of the world
Is justified to us.

PETER

And yet it's queer
To live like folks a million years ago.

NIMROD

Ay, there you hit it! But the Prophet's power
Was lost as long. The hearts of men, you've seen,
Are like their stomachs, used to this or that,
Shy of the best of food of other kind,
And some half starve before they taste of it.
Here you can aid: I need not tell you more:
There's ways of finding how a man inclines,
Without declaring much.

PETER

I understand.

NIMROD

The Prophet's soul is wrestling with his task.
Guard him from useless trouble, keep him free
From small disturbances! 'Tis much for you
To be a faithful watchman at his gates.

[*Exit.*

PETER

(*After a prolonged whistle.*)

It's half a pity such a man as that
Is out of Congress! When he means a thing,
It's safe to bet the thing will happen soon.
So *that's* the secret; and they're flustered both,
Misdoubting, doubtless, how the folks will take!
I'm mighty 'cute, when I lay out to be,
And here's good reason. Oh, I'll bait my hooks,
And jerk men's thoughts out, fast as hungry pike!
I'll go ahead where David wants to walk,
And cut a swath, then Jane and Mary Ann.

Scene IV.

The Council-Room. Nimrod Kraft *and the* Twelve *assembled.*

NIMROD

Nine out of twelve — thereto my voice the tenth —
Give clearest title: there's no room for doubt

(Which, as we stand, means nothing else than
fear);
For each, in silent seeking, urged by none,
By none persuaded, found the truth. We meet—
Against all secret understanding guard—
Declare in writing: speaks the Lord, or not?
Who else hath made so many of one mind?
And if the Prophet's light indeed be ours,
Shed on the law he means to give us next,
'Tis as a chosen field should plough itself,
So eager for the seed!

SIMEON

Who are the three?

HUGH

The question tells where you belong, at least.

NIMROD

They know; so shall the Prophet; 'tis enough!
The temple's dedication, now at hand,

Demands relaying of a basis built
Of what came nearest. Thin and crumbling stones
Must be removed, and those of solid grain
Replace them; 'twas intended from the first.

JONAS

I make no secret of dissent. Your words
Imply a threat: so speak it honestly!

NIMROD

Dissent may live, while disobedience dies.
I did not threaten: it may be myself
Shall be rejected first. If you require
The human logic of the call divine,
To settle new misgivings, none will blame,
So, afterwards, acceptance follows.

MORDECAI

Lord,
Enlighten them that wander in the dark!

SIMEON

So near accordance, let us cease to strive!
The law we pray for gives new power to man,
Takes old reproach from woman, multiplies
Inheritors of truth, as born therein,
And heals perversions that distress the world.
Oh, may it come!

JONAS

Yes; come to tear down homes,
And leave us tents instead, pitched wide apart!

NIMROD

Even so they dwelt; for Zion was their home;
And thereunto they gave what you deny,
The riches of their loins. Make end of talk:
The Prophet waits. Go, Simeon, bid him here!

[*Exit* SIMEON. *Immediately afterwards* DAVID *enters, and takes his seat at the head of the table.*]

DAVID

If I foresaw the form of your desire,
I left you, none the less, uninfluenced prayer,
And ample freedom. Whither tend your minds?

NIMROD

One here impeaches my sincerity:
Let Mordecai declare!

MORDECAI

We ten are one.
Three choose another sign, or ours distrust.
We would restore that patriarchal home
The Lord preferred, — its fair, obedient wives,
Its heritage of children; as He gave,
So giving now, that none be left alone
Or fruitless: thus the chasms of Gentile life
Wherein they fall, or pine on either side,
Shall all be closed in us.

DAVID

This makes a chasm
Impassable between us and the world.
Have you considered?

SIMEON

They that follow you
Already crossed, and hurled the bridges down.

NIMROD

Such test were all too easy. In our hearts,
By long transmission of the narrower love
Made shrunken, is the field of sacrifice.
Who offers there, in cheerful company
With her who for her sisters' sake submits,
And for the Lord's high pleasure, hath prevailed,
Forgets that he has ever lived ere now
(Thus you commanded), and is surely blessed,
Save bankrupt be the treasury of Heaven.

DAVID

Oh! send us, Lord, Thy keenest tongues of fire
To burn out reason, greed, and appetite,
And leave clear gold, the knowledge of Thy will.
There's truth in your concurrence; there is faith
That loves a trial; yea, so much as this
Lies, as a tree, within our planted seed.
But — in His own good time! What I declare —
Believe me, brethren! — comes through sore travail
Of mind and spirit: I am set as one
Beneath deep waves, who, looking for the day,
Sees watery lights, and ever-shifting gleams,
Till, in a calm betwixt the billowy tides,
The sun a moment pierces. Press not close:
The purest counsel may confuse us here.
Look ye, how many hearts are frozen yet,
Which, until thawed, must be withheld from fire!
But if — Nay, this is all. I charge you, wait!
On mine own soul I take the stress of yours,

To climb therewith: a finger stretched to help
May shake the balance: stand aside, and wait!

Scene V.

A room in the Prophet's *house.*

DAVID

(*Walking up and down.*)

I felt it come: within me and without
The signs agreed. One influence said, "Postpone!"
But something else — what was, what is it? — cries,
"No cowardice! the leaven of the world
Works in thy nature." Yet the inner sense, —
So pure it seems, even set against His light,
So simply strong, where old, insidious lust
May otherwise find entrance, — yea, it makes
Me coward! Here might woman offer help,
Had she but reached that statelier modesty

Which takes all mysteries of love and life
As God's enactments.

RHODA

(*Entering.*)

You have walked so long!
Your face is vexed with thought. What is it fills
The very air? I have forborne to ask,
Knowing the burden of the fate of all
Weighing upon you; yet, if those are right
Who counsel most, so soon to be relieved.

DAVID

It is not that, or only in such wise
As manifest direction of the past
And present blessing may increase the load.
For triumph makes afraid: it stings and stirs
All sleeping evil to a new assault;
Yet flatters so the self-exalted soul,

That what descended seems to dwell within.
They hope a further message, and with right:
The time is ripe; but whether purified
As who accepts a truth re-making life,
Or half with us, and half, unconsciously,
Swayed by an ancient conscience —

[*He pauses.*

RHODA.

Dare the truth,
As first you dared. I know no other law
Than I have learned of you.

DAVID

There spoke my wife!
Yea, if all women were so sweetly strung
To trust and follow us, the task were light.

RHODA

The women? How? you doubt their equal faith?

DAVID

(*Slowly, walking up and down, and closely watching* RHODA.)

Not equal faith, but equal — shall I say —
Self-abnegation? Nay, the word escapes.
'Tis one to either sex, yet opposite;
For man accepts, without a harm to love,
What unto woman seems its fatal hurt.
Such were not those of old, the strong and proud,
The stately mothers, favorites of the Lord.
What wife was Rachel, when she Bilhah gave?
Who now would yield, to multiply our tribe,
And take reproach from others, nuptial right?

RHODA

I fear to understand. Who asks the "right"?
What men demand the license? Surely you
Denied them?

DAVID

Wherefore use unseemly words?
Faith is not license, save in nobler sense;
And prayerful questioning is no demand.
Say "revelation," clear as any given:
Should this confirm, what then?

RHODA

'Twill not be given,
To strike the life from all true women's hearts!
Nay, hear me, David! Do not turn your face.
You are so good! They have misled your mind,
Those two, themselves misled, who cannot reach
Your purer height; but this is not of you.
Were we alone, and some strange sacrifice —
'Tis foolish, speaking thus! Put me aside,
But think of innocent wives, whose joy of life,
So satisfied with trust in one man's truth,
Sustains them in long weariness and fear,

That end in pangs, and endless, narrowing cares:
No, no: you will not rob them!

DAVID

Have I robbed
All these of home, to leave them shelterless?
Of ignorant faith, to send no power instead?
If care be less for each, yet love remain
Enough for all, I give, not take away.
To set her delicate heart in common breasts,
And so interpret, is a woman's way:
Were all as you are — Nay, there's little good
Conjecturing thus: I have a single path.
Shall He desert me, after glorious signs
Given from the first? Why, that undoes my work!
Who was it sent me to the wilderness,
Unsealed mine ears until the distant voice
Drew nearer, and a vision of the night
So seized and shook my helpless human soul,

That breath forsook me? Yea, almost I brake
The spider's thread dividing earth and heaven;
But such was not His will. When morning came,
And, lapped in faint indifference to life
I lay, the barren rock before mine eyes
Was as a table, spread by angel-hands!
He gave me food: I ate, and I was saved.
As well refuse the food he offers now,
And let faith, starving, die!

RHODA

(*Eagerly.*)

Who saved you then
May save again! 'Tis nought to offer food;
But I obeyed a voice, this moment clear,
And charged, I feel, with all the Lord's high will
In woman manifest. I pray you, take,
Even from my hands, which then were hid from you,
Now, openly, my evidence from Him!

DAVID

What double sense is in your words? I hear,
Not comprehending.

RHODA

How could I refrain?
Two days had passed: I dared not interrupt
Your solitude of soul, and prayers that fed
Upon the life of your forgotten frame;
But, guided near you, oh, thank Him for that!
I left the food —

DAVID

You? you!

RHODA

As was His will.
What ails you, David?

[*Aside.*]

He is deadly pale;

There's something fierce and strange within his
eyes:
He frightens me.

DAVID

You brought me food?

RHODA

I did.

DAVID

What else? What more have you in secret done?
Who taught you so to counterfeit the Lord?
Woman! to burrow underneath my feet,
And make a hollowness where rock should be!
How dared you cheat me?

RHODA

Slay me with your hand,
Not with such face and words! If I but saved
(You say it saved you), how could love refrain?

I have obeyed, believed all else in you,
As I believe and worship still: forgive!

[*She falls on her knees before him.*

DAVID

Not unto me, your husband, David, man;
But, if I be a Prophet of the Lord,
Yes, *if!* It seems to you a little thing:
Rise up! I cannot answer now: the house
Rocks to and fro, the temple's pinnacles
Dance in the air like devils' shuttlecocks:
There's nothing stable. Rise, I say again!

[*She rises to her feet.*]

Now take your seat, and sew! I've heard it said
Women think better when the hand's employed:
If 'tis so, think!

[*He moves towards the door.*

RHODA

David!

DAVID

I go to pray.

[*Exit.*

RHODA

Come back! He's gone. O God! what have I done?

Scene VI.

Midnight. The interior of the temple: a row of columns, on either side of the nave, throws the side aisles into shadow. A huge baptismal font of stone, resting on four rudely-sculptured figures, — a lion, an ox, a griffin, and a ram, — rises from the floor: behind, on a platform of stone, an altar bearing the ark, on each side of which lights are burning in seven-branched candlesticks. A veil, partly lifted on one side, conceals a semicircular chancel, which is the Holy of Holies.

DAVID

(*Slowly pacing along the nave.*)

And this complete, a house to give Him joy!
So near, so great, the triumph, and the dread

Forerunning it! But, while I feared a bolt
From heaven, the earth, without a warning, heaved.
She cannot see the harm, nor I translate:
O doubt of soul, so often trampled down!
O highest faith, as oft renewed in pain!
Why comes your fiercest battle now? *She* fed;
An accident upset the toppling rock;
The vision was a dream: the flock I lead
Is fooled by me, as I have fooled myself!
Howe'er I turn, I stand as girt by fire;
And all in me which seemed divinely good
Is changed to poison, made a scorpion-sting,
To pierce my soul with death. Oh, hearken, Lord!

[*He buries his face in his hands. A shadow glides swiftly from pillar to pillar, and pauses opposite to him.*]

LIVIA

(*Aside, in a whisper.*)

He's nigh despair: I know — there's but one source —

Whence comes it. Fail me not, my woman's
heart,
Or he and I are lost.

DAVID

(*Lifting his head.*)

He will not speak!
Doth He not know how terrible it is
To ask, and not be answered? Why, one soul,
For sin so tortured, would make justice weep;
But this is good, this seek a million souls.
What, then, is He? Hold, hold! There lies a
gulf
Whose awful darkness frightens worse than flame.
The thought's a serpent, coiled round heart and
throat,
And crushing life, save one dull spark that burns
In suffering only.

[*He staggers to one side, and leans against a column.*

LIVIA

(*Aside.*)

This is deepest woe
Of doubt, that vibrates back to faith again,
Can I but loose the string. He must not see,
Nor hear, as yet; but, stay! one chance remains.

[*She steals forward, and vanishes in the darkness.*

DAVID

Thus all accomplished crumbles, slides away!
Power lost, authority's a puff of smoke;
Respect becomes its angry opposite;
For each an insult in my failure feels,
Spying a cold intention where I gave
In self-forgetting faith.

This dare not be:
Am I set back, to seek His face again?
Through heat and haste of youth, too ardent hope
Of large acceptance, was confusion born,

And still I stray? Even for the sake of men,
Should I appear as I believed I was?
One line of light, — one little entering thread,
As through a worm-hole in a shutter probes
A darkened chamber, — that would save my power.

[*The bass-pipes of the organ begin to sound, scarcely audible at first, but gradually increasing in volume; then, after a few simple, alternating chords, a faint, flute-like stop is added.*]

Is this an answer, out of weary sense
Awakened, to delude me as before?
Not so! I cannot dream such harmonies:
That shuddering of the air, that far-off sweep
Of myriad voices, hiding what they sing, —
I feel, I hear again! Come near, and speak!
Fold up your fluttering wings, that shake the sound,
Or soothe my passion, loosened through the eyes,
Till I distinguish. Oh! some pity breathes

In your celestial sweetness, melting me
To such self-sorrow, I can bear no more.

[*He covers his face, and weeps: the music gradually ceases.*]

My soul is quieted, and yet so sad!
It seems to wait, not all disclothed of hope,
But passive, like the silence of a child
Shut up alone, whom love may soon release.
But I, — will love release me?

LIVIA

(*Stepping noiselessly forward: in a low voice.*)

Prophet, yea!

DAVID

(*Starting.*)

Ah! What is this? How came you here?

LIVIA

He called.

DAVID

He called? What said He?

LIVIA

First, "Prepare a chant,
Meet for the dedication of My house."
I rose, came hither; and the organ-stops
Compelled my fingers to the strain you heard.
As in a dream, the solemn, breathing chords
Filled all of space beneath the hollow sky,
Above a valley; trees and rocky crests
I seemed to see; and one awaiting soul
Was there, and listening.

DAVID

Livia! This you saw?

LIVIA

Dimly, and far away; but you were near.
Within the temple something wild and strange,

A sense of agony, a dread appeal,
So pierced my soul, I wept. I felt whence came
The subtile influence, — felt, and yielded all
Receptive tablets of magnetic sense
Which woman keeps, the substitute for power;
Till what, unconsciously, you wrote thereon
Brought me to you.

DAVID

I wrote? and you know all?
'Twere miracle! and yet, within your eyes
I read the knowledge.

LIVIA

Also that my faith
Finds surer triumph, planted in your doubt?
This is the prophet-nature: such were they
Whose lips became live coals of kindled truth,
Dipped in the hell of an uncertain mind,

To fit them for the bliss of certainty.
What you esteem more keenly, dreading loss,
You will attain: your very fears are hopes;
For, if the signs of power be accidents,
Then accident is greater miracle!

DAVID

Ha!

LIVIA

Thus, each side, your feet are firmly set.

DAVID

And what I ponder, — is it known to you?

LIVIA

Ay, known and pondered, as a woman weighs
Her share in law, her half of destiny;
Not coldly, but with warm, impressive mind,
That shapes its living features. Would you see
Their form in mine?

DAVID

I feel it, ere you speak;
And yet I would behold.

LIVIA

Within my heart
Truth purer is, than educated shame.
Unteach this last in woman, she will love
Not selfishly, as now, — possessing less
By claiming more, — but with a proud content
In yielding home and honor to the rest.

[*She speaks in a lower tone.*]

Here might I help: my heart suggests a way
It shrinks from, save extremity of need
Demand all sacrifice. If I confess
One timid prayer, and justify the law
Through my desire, I do but shut the door
On its fulfilment.

DAVID

Livia!

LIVIA

Bid me speak,
And by obedience other bliss may come.

DAVID

Livia! fulfilment of your prayer, and mine!
So many hearts, as birds in mating-time,
Draw near each other perched on hedge and spray;
But ours, like skylarks, met above the cloud!
When first I saw you, there was touch of wings,
Far up in loftier solitudes of air
A warm companionship. You cannot sink
Below our partnèred light, nor I, alone,
Aspire beyond it. Come, and be yourself
The law, the revelation!

[*He stretches out his arms:* LIVIA *throws herself upon his breast.*]

LIVIA

David! now
My Prophet and my love!

[*Kissing him.*]

Oh! nevermore
Shall I, thus beckoned, falter on the way;
But when your weary spirit leans on mine,
And draws such life as once, from hers he gave,
The Roman father, I am all fulfilled.
This is the place, the purpose, and the power
For me ordained: be not less bold to take
Than I to give!

DAVID

(*Returning her kisses.*)

This sign shall triumph. Lo!
The Enemy but made his last assault:
My power comes back: the temple stands complete!

SCENE VII.

Midnight. A bed-chamber in the PROPHET'S *house.* RHODA *seated near a small table, upon which is a shaded lamp; the New Testament in her lap; the child asleep in a crib near her.*

RHODA

(*Closing the volume.*)

It is not there; or else my troubled mind
Fails to detect it. All the precious words,
All, all, I find; that, like a mother's kiss
And healing breath upon her baby's hurt,
Make the poor heart forget its bruise, — all, all!
The sweetness of the Life that loved the world,
So hallowing human love; the promises
That keep a nobler justice still alive
Beneath each wrong; the nearness of the Lord,
As of a wing that covers and defends, —
They shine upon me. Only this unsaid?

He *must* have said it: they forgot to write.
It was so small a thing for Him, — ten words
To help all women, — yea, enough were three!
A single breathing from His lips divine,
And we were saved; for, though he meant so much,
Not thus commanding, men will dare deny!

I saw the text so clearly in my soul, —
Already marked, and laid the open book
On David's desk. He could not help but see,
And then the power within him would be firm,
I prayed, to conquer other counsel. Ah!
What course remains? My tongue deceives my heart;
I speak but foolishness, and vex him more.
But hers makes beautiful a darkened thought,
Makes purity a secret selfishness,
And holy love an evil. Oh, 'tis false!

Why, whât did he declare me at the first? —
That faith and love are one! Give me a line,
Clear, pointed, piercing, from the armory here,
And I will use it as a sword. I reach,
But they are hung too high, or over-weight
My hand; and I am helpless to contend,
As if the Lord opposed me.

[*The child moves restlessly in his sleep.*]

You are safe,
My baby, even from the world's reproach, —
Of love begotten, ere its nature strayed.
What waits for you and me? Confusion comes
When that which in the universal heart
Alone is holy finds no reverence.

[*The child wakens, and begins to cry. She takes him from the crib, folds him warmly in the bed-clothes, and rocks him upon her breast.*]

Hush, darling, hush! If that thy mother's woe
Hath pierced thine innocent, unconscious rest,

And wakened thee in witless trouble, hush!
Thou art too young for any thing but joy,
Too dear for shadowed pain; and some old song
Must cheat my sorrow till thou sleep'st again.

[*Sings.*]

"My baby smiles, at last awake:
The curtains let me draw,
And on my happy bosom take
The child he never saw.

"He'll come to-night: the wind's at rest,
The moon is full and fair;
I wear the dress that pleased him best,
A ribbon in my hair.

"So lately wed, so long away!
But, oh! between is joy:
He left a wife; he'll find to-day
A mother and a boy.

"Be still, my heart! the sound I hear
Is not the step I know;
But hope so perfect turns to fear,
And bliss is nigh to woe.

"What voices now delay his tread,
  Or plan a sweet surprise?
Come, babe! and we shall wake, instead,
  The rapture of his eyes."

The moonlight, through the open door,
  Upon her forehead smiled.
Still feet and frozen heart they bore:
  He never saw his child!

[*She breaks into a passion of weeping.*

ACT IV.

SCENE I. — THE TEMPLE.

Grand ceremony of dedication: the main aisle is thronged with people, — men, women, and children. The baptismal font is filled with water, and decorated with garlands. Lights are burning in the seven-branched candlesticks: a flat brazier, containing live coals, stands upon the altar. The Holy of Holies is concealed by a dark purple veil. Upon the platform, in the centre, on the right hand of the altar, stands DAVID, *in robes of white, embroidered with gold; on the left hand,* NIMROD KRAFT, *as high-priest, in robes of violet, embroidered with silver, and a tall silver mitre upon his head; behind them ten members of the* COUNCIL OF TWELVE, *in robes of pale green, bordered with crimson: they bear symbols, representing the gifts and attributes of the Church. Four boys, standing below, in front of the altar, hold censers in their hands.*

DAVID

This having heard, — commanded to receive,
By Him who speaks through me, — do you possess
As somewhat, unto them whose hearts are strong
To plant His service in devoted lives,
Permitted; not as ordered unto all.
The sword of Truth is only terrible
Against defiant wills: whoso obeys
In spirit, though his human reason fail,
Shall yet perceive in spirit, and be glad.
It is the highest faith that tramples down
Rebellious intellect: while this is blind,
That sees; and even where the softer heart
May tremble, in its delicate habit jarred
By harmonies of love that first disturb,
'Tis Faith that soothes our bosom's frightened bird,
And says, "The nestlings and the nest are safe."
Remember this; and still exalt your souls
To light that purifies, while fancied warmth

May stream from darkness. That revealed, I give;
Not that expected, or of men preferred.
And Thou who gavest, symbol of whose truth
These living coals upon Thine altar glow,
Take, from the hands of the anointed priest,
Our first burnt-offering! As it melts in flame,
And radiance out of darkened dross is born,
So melt from us, in this Thy holy house,
All understanding, feeling, thought, and love
Not meet for Thee, till every soul, refined,
Burn in an upward glory.

NIMROD

If strange fire,
Hated of Thee, the food of heathen gods,
Come forth from what we offer, quench the flame,
Or turn it back, consuming these my hands!

[*With both hands he casts something upon the coals. A clear, rose-colored flame arises, steadily increasing in brilliancy, until all the interior of the temple is tinted by its radiance. The boys swing their censers; and the clouds of perfumed smoke are illuminated as they rise.*]

CHANT

(*With full organ accompaniment.*)

Hosanna! harp and song
  Proclaim the consummation:
Homeless on earth so long,
  Thou hast an habitation!
As was of old Thy bid,
Thine holy place is hid:
Descend, and dwell amid
  Thy chosen nation!
Hark to the voice of Thy welcome, Jehovah!

Make this Thy city proud,
  And this Thy sacred river!
Guard us with fire and cloud,
  And arrows from Thy quiver!
Increase us where we stand,
That we possess the land;
And from our enemy's hand
  With might deliver!
Dwell in the house we have builded, Jehovah!

JONAS

(*Among the congregation, to* Hugh.)

The most are caught. I marvel at myself,
Like one, who, entering on a company
Filled with deceitful wine, tongues thawed and
hearts,
Feels an unfriendly soberness of blood,
Until their folly rights him. This alone
Were harmless luxury for stinted souls,
Save for its rootage in their homely lives.
The evil waxes strong.

HUGH

And weak, thereby,
Our chances. Note the women's faces, here!
At first I thought them troubled: now the bait,
Self-sacrifice, upon the hook of faith,
But gently frightens: they already feel
Consent approach, and shyly play with it,
To gulp more perfectly at last.

JONAS

Be still!
The priest, through all his haze of sanctity,
Fails not to watch us: meet me three days hence.

NIMROD

(*Addressing the people.*)

Even as He charged, sojourning in the coasts
Of Gadara, tell no man this ye saw.
Who came to us must their belief attest,
Ere they be worthy of the signs. Dull ears
Misread the revelations: clouded eyes
Behold them darkly. Wherefore, you that know,
Be as enclosèd gardens to the world.
The highway is no Tabor, meet for saints;
The market-place is no Gethsemane.
Keep the exceeding nearness of the Lord,
This day, and when again in voice and flame
He visits us, like secret holiness

We share as brethren, but none else than we.
I gave you once the Prophet's parable,
Here verified: the tender roots of faith,
That feed such glorious summer-leaves of life,
Lie deep below, and wither when laid bare.
A happy bond, indeed, is speech of that
Which moves the heart; but holier, sweeter far,
The bond of silence, guarding truth revealed!

MORDECAI

(*To* SIMEON.)

Wise words, and most devout! But wherefore now
Adds he this law, when, publishing the first,
We gather thousands?

SIMEON.

Not to any one
May I declare, even that I know his mind.
I say not that I know it: be assured,
No less, that also wisdom orders here.

DAVID

(*To the people.*)

Once more my mouth is opened ere ye go.
In every house the fatness of our land
Prepares your feast; the shawms and sackbuts wait,
With lighter measures, for rejoicing feet;
The day is made a glory, far and wide,
On shore and river. Issuing forth to these,
Let not your perfect exaltation sink
Even to the gladsome level of the time.
Behold in all, as out of nothing wrought,
What here the soul commanded, and the hand,
A willing slave, fulfilled! As it hath been,
So, with increasing forces, let it be;
And, from the loins of us that humbly serve,
Shall start the lineage of millennial kings!

[*Sound of the organ. The* PROPHET, HIGH-PRIEST, *and members of the* TWELVE *come forward to the front of the platform, and lift their hands, while the people gradually disperse.*]

Scene II.

A room in the house of Jonas. *Night. A small lamp burning upon the table; the shutters closed.* Jonas, *his wife* Sarah, Hugh, *and* Hiram, *a member of the Church.*

SARAH

Walls hear, 'tis said; but they've no tongues to blab.
Up street and down, so far as I can see,
'Tis lonely as a graveyard: use your chance,
And well, and quickly!

JONAS

Many more are ripe
For what we may determine: all they need
Is certainty of equal power opposed;
And this, within the compass of our flock,
They see not, neither is it found: so strong,
So as with Devil's wisdom skilled to work,

Is Nimrod Kraft. But one thing hath he taught
Whereby we profit, — to keep counsel close,
Direction in a single pair of hands,
And move, when ready, backed by secret force.
Why, such a man profanes conspiracy,
So using it! His weapons, in our hands,
Scoured by the better purpose, are made sure.

HUGH

The hands are yours that shape the counter-plan;
And mine are idle till you bid them do.
Whence comes the equal power?

SARAH

If men are weak,
Then women easily may foil the law.
It were the rarest show, good faith! to see
The battle left to us; our recompense,
To own their weakness whole, which, but for us,
Would be divided.

JONAS

Nay, you haste too much.
Already half the leaven of discontent
Is kneaded up in their submissive clay;
And that which drew us, and we still accept,
Grows one with what we loathe. Thus open war
Were vainly ventured: leaving them, we lose
Possession and its chances. What remains?
The help abiding in the outer law, —
A hand still stretched, to smite where it forbids,
As this, yet spare whatever else we hold.

HUGH

Then, as I guess, you guide the Gentile law
To his confusion only? Can you stay
Its meddling there, nor open other pleas,
Which, in the end, may set us where we stood
At the beginning?

JONAS

There my secret lies.
The world is pressing on us: right and left
New colonies have passed the prairie lands,
To settle on the river-bluffs, and build
Some cabin-city they believe shall be
A centre of the world. The chief of one,
And potent in their county government,
Is kin of mine; and messages have passed.
That half the plot, and most of danger, falls
To them who work outside, not seeming leagued,
Demands advantage. What were ours to give,
After success, and what were fair to give, —
So that the leadership secures to us, —
Needs final parley: time and place are fixed.

HIRAM

As here and now declared: this day I bore
Your message and its answer. Colonel Hyde

Sees lighter work in leading on his men
Than holding back: the excitement grows apace.
Give evidence to make pretence of law
A legal movement, should the law inquire:
He asks no more.

HUGH

The revelation, say?

JONAS

Just that! With all the priest's freemasonry
To keep the usage secret, here and there
Are leaky souls: the raftsmen, as they pass
The landing; firemen, wooding up their boats;
Or peddling agents, prowling through the land,—
Catch hints of it, and bear disfigured forth.
Thus interference threatens either way;
But we avert a ruin possible,
And seat ourselves in power, to change and save,
By pointing the attack.

HUGH

And yet I've heard
How one, that, in the guns against him fired,
Had rammed blank cartridges, forgot a ball.
Your plan is perfect, if the guidance holds —

SARAH

(*Interrupting him.*)

What man are you, to fear the lesser risk?
The thing is coming. Standing now to us,
You lose no more, though interference fail,
And gain by any change.

JONAS

The fact of kin
In him whose hands must grapple with the priest
Is my security. Full match is he,
As you shall know. We meet, to settle all,
Beyond the river-bend, just where the bluff

Turns inland, and the little brook comes down.
'Tis thickly wooded: there the Indians made
Their final stand; and rows of bleaching ribs
Shine, like the fangs of steel-traps, from the grass.
Even border hunters, bold to hug a bear,
Avoid it after nightfall: we are safe
From even suspicion's ear, conferring there.
Will you go with me?

HUGH

Coward am I not,
Though cautious, as befits a man full-grown.
But woman's virtue caution never was:
Only the rash are brave to her. I'll go!

Scene III.

Night. A street in the city.

HUGH

(*Walking slowly homewards.*)

Were he alone, he might conspire alone,
And welcome! This is shrewdly done, if his;
The more, if hers. I thought her not so wise.
If interference menaces indeed,
And one might make conditions, then, why, then
Comes chance to seize o'erthrown authority, —
No matter whose, — and let it stick to me.
So much there is of wisdom in the plan:
We lose by quiet, and we can but gain
By new disturbance. Had he promised aught —
But 'tis the same! What as an offer fails,
Can I exact: which side goes up or down,
One moment both are balanced evenly,
And then a hand decides. The man's a fool

Who thinks to cheapen revolution's cost,
And feed enthusiasm upon itself,
Without the hope of benefit: go to!
I may be made a cat's-paw, but sharp-eyed
To grab one chestnut, — let me see it first!

NIMROD

(*Suddenly appearing at his side.*)

I'll show you! What! you meditate escape?
Stand still! I will not touch you, since you must.
How left you Jonas?

HUGH

In his usual mood;
Dissenting, yet not disobedient.

NIMROD

And yours the same? Should I repeat his words,
While every tone is in your ears alive,

You would deny them: so I waste no breath.
I would have suffered you to take the lead
To that fair quicksand-scum you think is turf,
And said, "Good riddance!" — save that you can serve;
And that you *will*, is truth, when I declare
You shall not serve unpaid.

HUGH

A Devil's brain
Is yours!

NIMROD

A brain that once he owned, perhaps;
Now by the Lord, to his discomfiture,
Tuned otherwise.

HUGH

(*Aside.*)

Why, even here, to me,
With both hands full of treachery and bribes,

He says such things! That's genius, on my
soul!

[*Aloud.*]

The Lord directs you? well, then, also me,
If I should do your will.

NIMROD

My instrument
Is surely His, in spite of halting faith.

HUGH

What would you have me do?

NIMROD

Stay what you are,
A traitor! plot and plan our overthrow,
With him and others: only, as a spout
Collects, from every shingle on the roof,
What rain it sheds, to fill the thirsty tank,
Convey to me your knowledge, me alone!

HUGH

The Lord commands at will what He forbids,
It seems, or you interpret loosely: be it so!
I'll grant His purpose better know to you,
And let you patch the breakage in His law;
But, if the open virtue earns reward,
This claims a higher payment!

NIMROD

In your work
Will soon be shown the form of your desire,
Which, being seen, I'll make reality.
Though partly known to me, I dare not speak
The Prophet's mind, but bid you ponder this:
If you were set aside, not faithless charged,
Nor any virtue lacking, but for use,
As one unjustly to conspiracy
Compelled, by justice to be beckoned back,
And crowned by honor when the plot is crushed,
How then?

HUGH.

(*Aside.*)

This is a touch beyond me! Driven,
While will and purpose wholly seemed my own,
To do the thing he wanted, — can it be?

(*Aloud.*)

"How then?" 'Tis just another miracle.
There have been men whose tongues or hands obeyed
Some dark, mysterious force, and did the things
Their souls resisted: am I one of such?

NIMROD

It well may be: the working of the power,
Itself is mystery. Weary not your mind,
As if to your account were aught set down,
Even seeming treachery. So much we know,
Source, pretext, object, chance, and means of aid,

That, had your virtue yielded, we were safe;
But time is gained since you endure the test,
And labor lessened. Here your service lies.
First, come with me, and state the very truth,
Mindful that, if you swerve, my knowledge waits
To prop your memory. This rehearsal made,
And duty fixed in what concerns us next,
We'll talk of your exaltment and reward.

[*Exeunt.*

Scene IV.

Livia's *house.* David *seated in a cushioned arm-chair:* Livia *on a low stool beside him.*

DAVID

The restlessness that stirs in feet and limbs,
The dull confusions that besiege the brain,
The strange uncertainties of heart, pass off
When you are near me: overhead in blue
The sun comes out; and life is like a land

Where tempered winds kiss buds, and make them
flowers.
What is your magic? Nay, it it is yourself!

LIVIA

It is that I, who follow and believe,
So spared the high anxieties of soul
In you that cleave your passage to the truth,
Am ever fresh, a little way beneath,
To stay your weariness from further fall.
The light your being brings transfuses mine
With strength and gladness ever to uphold
Myself, upholding you.

DAVID

The gift of tongues
If I bestowed, yet scarce the gift of song.
Whence come your hymns, as eloquent of faith
As Miriam sang, between the sea and Shur, —

Rejoicing strains, that suit our cheerful laws,
And shame the Gentiles' wailing psalmody?

LIVIA

'Tis consecration of a skill profane
Wherein my soul found foolish peace. I sang,
In that dark time before I saw your eyes,
Of knightly harps, and willow-wearing maids,
Of jewelled crowns, red swords, and evening stars,
And lonely tombs, and ghosts that wept and went.
One burden beat through all. Such songs betrayed
The lack of that which sweeter is than song,
Now found; but raptures of believing bliss
Seek the same passage, and the single voice,
Chanting in them, becomes the speech of all!
Stay, would you hear a ditty which yourself,
As one whose arm may brush accordant strings,
Nor mark in passing, did awake in me?
A secret, else, and dumb for other ears.

DAVID

Oh, sing! Though David's craft you exercise
In being silent, yet my soul demands.

LIVIA

(Takes a guitar from a table, tunes the strings, and after a soft, subduing prelude, sings.)

Let words be faint, and song refuse
To frame the speech divine:
Look on me, love, and all they lose
Your eyes shall sing to mine!
I ask no voice to breathe my bliss,
Or bid its answer come;
For lips are silent when they kiss,
And meeting hearts are dumb.

A wave that slides to clasp a wave,
On mine your being flows;
The pang you took, the peace you gave,
Must wed in such repose.
So, love, your eyes alone shall tell
What else were unconfessed;
And, if too fondly mine compel,
Oh, hide them on your breast!

DAVID

Livia! What are you? What triumphant force
Flows out from you, and knits my blood with yours?
How is it that the liquid dark of eyes
I gaze on grows a broadening sphere of light,
Enclosing me forever? — touching so
Your hand, that suddenly a warmer world
Beckons and wooes as if it might be mine? —
That in your cheek the blossom-tender flesh,
As it were spirit, sanctifies my lips?
Oh! you are beautiful.

LIVIA

Because I love!
All happiness prints beauty on the face.
I cannot keep it like a bridal-dress,
Laid in a drawer, with fragrant orris-root,
And wear my working-gowns again. I'm bold,
And proud of boldness, glad because of pride,

And love the more for gladness! Thus my heart
Beats in a ring, beginning as it ends, —
A magic circle, and you dwell therein!

DAVID

My love!

LIVIA.

You say it, and I echo back.
What more is freedom to a beaten slave,
Than this to me? Oh! I could sit, as now,
And study all the beauty of your eyes,
Where nameless color brightens here to blue,
And there turns brown, until the dusk should leave
Their sparkle only. I could part your locks,
And from my fingers shake their wandering gloss,
To seize again, and soothe with creeping thrills,
Till you should dip in slumber ere you knew.
I am as one that scarcely can believe

Past poverty is o'er, but ever spends,
To teach himself his hands are verily gold.
If you have feared, lest shame and danger wait
To blight the second marriage of your heart,
Leave me to meet them, and to tread them down.

DAVID

I fear no more; I wait no longer: come!

Scene V.

The Council-Room. David, Nimrod, Simeon, *and* Mordecai *in secret conference.*

DAVID

The danger's real: shut within our camp,
Would perfidy, in time, consume itself;
But thus, in league with outer ignorance
That easily breeds hate, it threatens harm.
Have you assured yourself how much of truth

In this alliance lies? — with how much power
It arms itself?

NIMROD

Last night my messengers
Came back from close espial of the land.
With tongues disguised to speak the Gentile mind,
They won so much as Colonel Hyde sees fit
To let his followers know; and strangely shows
Our Church's image in their looking-glass!
Hereof they speak: a faction needing help
Among us; hints of strange, unholy rites
To be suppressed; and promised evidence
(For he, considerate of future place,
First means to lift the banner of the law);
Then, last of all, his godless crew expects
Plunder and ravage! They would snatch away,
With unclean hands, the Lord's high heritage, —
They careful of the faith! The Devil laughs,
Methinks, to see such Christian volunteers

Assail our industry with hands of theft,
Our laws with sinful bodies, and our prayers
With tongues that cast defilement when they speak.

MORDECAI

Oh, sons of Belial! But the Lord shall raise
His hand to smite, as at the gates of Aï.

NIMROD

What have we done that should alarm their law?
Lo! strife and murder in this border land
It scarcely chides, is patient of free lust,
Yet makes a culprit of the sanctioned love
That broadens home. It waits for evidence.
I would not counsel rashness: let it wait,
And not receive!

DAVID

Then is their pretext vain;
For we, appealing to the selfsame source,

Possess law's shield, to hold against its sword
Wherewith they threaten. That were best of all;
But how prevent the tales, if true or false,
Which may be carried?

NIMROD

(*After a pause.*)

He who governs us
Once smote directly: will He do so now?
The liar once fell dead; the enemy
Was slaughtered, and no child of all his seed
Renewed the race: even mercy was reproach,
And Moses felt the anger of the Lord,
When human plea persuaded him to spare.
How much the more than what was punished thus
Doth Jonas purpose! Why delays the bolt?
Why rusts the blade in God's closed armory?
Or, waits He for our call? means He to test
What zeal and courage guard His holy place?

Then, cry aloud! As it was said of old,
They were not, for the Lord had taken them,
So in your soul command, Let him not be!

SIMEON

Ay! that were shortest passage to the end:
Let him not be!

MORDECAI

Who from the Anakim
His hosts delivered, over Arnon led,
And gave the men of Heshbon to their hands,
Will, from exceeding smallness of this prayer,
Be merry in His mind! No giants here
Oppose our path, but one malicious dwarf,
Whose pointed tongue may verily stab to hurt:
Let him not be!

DAVID

If some mysterious ail,
Even while we speak, should palsy all his frame,

Yea, stop with sudden check the wheels of life,
The thing were good; but thus to stretch a
 hand,
And beckon, consciously, the fate on watch—
Why should it seem so different? What sense
Makes us so thoughtless when we plant a life,
Knowing the awful sanctity it holds,
When we would take away? Yet, if life serve,
Fulfilling as it may His will in man,
Then why not death?

[*He pauses, looks upwards with an expression of profound abstraction, and continues, as if speaking to himself.*]

I see the poor beast's eyes,
And that tremendous question hid in them,
I tried to answer. Like a human life
I loved the dog's; but when the other came,
With certain madness in his slavering jaws,
And sprang upon and bit and tumbled him,

Then staggered forward, seeking where to die,
My hands were armed with pitying cruelty;
And he, so doomed, forefeeling all his doom,
Crouched down, and, whimpering, read some fatal
change
Set in my face: the liquid, lustrous eyes,
So sad with yearning after human speech,
With love that never can declare itself,
So tender, now so wild with dumb despair,
Implored in vain: it was a tragedy,
O God! and I the unrelenting fate.
'Twas kindness, in the shape of monstrous guilt
Disguised; and, for his sake and mine, I prayed
That, through continuous being, he might know
And pardon.

Even so doth God prevent?
Is moral madness, some implanted seed
Of harm to all, thus hindered in our lives,

Though by the uncomprehended blow should bleed
A thousand loving hearts? I thought so then.
It seems not much, when such an aim demands:
"Let him not be!" The words themselves seduce
With seeming innocence, — and each a stab:
"Let him not be!"

[*Nimrod makes a sign to Simeon and Mordecai, who steal quietly out of the Council-Room.*]

I shrink from asking that
Which in my secret soul I hope may come:
Why should I shrink? The days wherein we live
Allow no Moses-nature; but for him
The Lord descended, counselled face to face,
And hallowed slaughter with direct command.
Am I so far from ancient holiness,
I dare not pray His hand should touch the man
Who plots my ruin? How bring, otherwise,

Conditions which make sure the covenant?
Here lies a *must:* it calls me to subdue
My frightened fancy, and forget the heart
Which tries to make itself accomplice: yes,
I will implore *His* vengeance,—but no more.

NIMROD

And should He answer, as my faith expects,
The prayer is justified unto your soul.
Your dread is but the birth-pang of the law
Reborn in you; and when in living flesh
It smiles, and waxes strong, you will forget
All save the glory.

DAVID

Be your words fulfilled!
The thing you counselled is already done.
What in the soul one fleeting moment stands
Is asked beyond recall: let us go hence!

[*Exeunt.*

Scene VI.

A narrow, wooded ravine between bluffs crowned with rock. Late twilight. Jonas *and* Hugh *under a tree.*

HUGH

(*Aside, looking around him.*)

A pokerish place! There's something in the air
Breeds thoughts of murder; and I'm cold with creeps
That pinched my flesh, from stepping on a spine,
Wherefrom the skull, so loosened, rolled away.
Were but the business done!

(*Aloud.*)

He's in no haste,
Or we too hasty: he outstays the time.
Once more reflect upon the thing you do:
Is it well done?

JONAS

I settled that at first.
There's safety in surprise: if Nimrod guessed
The range of popular impatience, then,
I grant you, were some hazard to be met.
But he is idle, seeks additional wives,
And feels as certain of the power he holds
As doth a man of money in his fist,
While at his back the robber's club is raised
To stretch him dumb.

HUGH

A strong comparison!

JONAS

It suits his case. You think I underrate
The man's intelligence; why, not a whit!
Our lucky chance is his security,
Which we must use before a breath disturb.

[*A low whistle is heard.*]

The Colonel's signal!

[*He whistles in answer.*]

Mark you, when he comes,
How perfectly he understands his work,
And sets all parts together till they fit!
That's where the lawyer tells.

COLONEL HYDE

(*Approaching.*)

Good even to both!
Your friend this, Cousin Jonas? Here's my hand;
And now, to business! Something must be done,
If done at all, before the week is out,—
That is, as you and I, and this your friend,
Desire to happen: something else is sure.
The excitement grows; and soon your priest, forewarned,
Will organize resistance; then comes war

To waste the property we want to save.
Have you the evidence? A document
Were best; but witnesses will answer here.

JONAS

The written revelation which he read
Was laid within the ark: that you must seize,
And bear away; resistance then will stop.
Our witness must be forced, unwillingly,
After arrest: I bring you here the names
Of them who can be driven to testify.
You understand?

COLONEL HYDE

If they the practice prove!
The revelation shows intent, no more,
And violates no law.

JONAS

To all of these
The fact is patent: where you need one case,
We give you five.

COLONEL HYDE

As fingers of a hand
That soon shall clutch them! 'Tis enough for law,
Which started, many accidents may chance
Before the process finds a legal stop.
And now, conditions! You demand the power;
I, its equivalent, a part secured,
A part reserved for possible future need,
So you gain influence—

JONAS

And you assure
The chance of power! Neither can promise all.

HUGH

(*Aside.*)

Where two so bargain, there's not margin left
To hold a third.

COLONEL HYDE

The time for huckstering's gone.

JONAS

Missing my aim, comes little; winning, all!

COLONEL HYDE

Then here's an end of parley: let us go!
This is no place for pleasure.

JONAS

So, farewell!
Your stipulations hang on my success.

[*Exit* COLONEL HYDE.]

Come, Hugh! the night is cloudy: I must seek,
More with my feet than eyes, the ticklish path.

[*He moves away.*

HUGH

Go on, but slowly. I have dropped my knife,
And look for 't with my hands. Before you reach

The slippery corner where we climb the bluff,
I'll overtake you.

[JONAS *disappears in the gloom.*]

Shall I overtake
Indeed? I'm not so sure: yes, Colonel Hyde,
An accident, if prayed for, might occur!
They told me nothing; but the gift of guess
Remains to me; and, ugh! 'tis horrible.
I'll neither see nor know! The skull I kicked,
Used as a pillow, would not breed such dreams.

[*He moves onward, cautiously.*]

Ha! what was that? Along the darkened path
Something, still darker, moves! I hear no sound,
And yet the silence seems a piercing cry!
I feel the lifting of my hair: I'll stop
Both ears, shut eyes, and think of any thing,
Till I can count ten thousand, then, go on!

Scene VII.

A room in the Prophet's *house.*

DAVID

No, you are not the same! The simple trust
Which found content in what I was — and this
Includes whatever more I am become —
Hath left your eyes: your tongue is silenter:
You speak but matters which compel your speech,
And in your ways make hints of things unsaid.
I say not this in blame: you cannot be
More than you are, or other: I had hoped
There were a force in faith, a warmth in love,
To hold your nature side by side with mine,
And take a larger property in me
Through that which only seems to lessen it.
My hope is vain.

RHODA

Oh! wait a little while,
My husband, — as you still and ever are.
I vexed you sore in what I thought was good,
And that seems evil which you ask of me:
It was not so at first. I lean on you
With all my weight; when you would rest, in turn,
I've nothing but my simple, loving heart,
To stay your weariness. I cannot urge
Your spirit forward on its loftier ways;
Nor did you ask it, save my faith be aid,
When first we loved. Take what another brings:
You will not find me selfish: take so much,
But keep your heart for me.

DAVID

Why, it is yours,
No less than then! A very ghost of change

Is what you fancy. Shut your eyes, and call
My face into your memory: 'tis the same.

RHODA

Ah, David, David! I would shut their sight
Forever, could you in my ears again
So live. There's something in a woman's heart,
I think, so delicate, so soft a force,
That it will cling like steel, nor feel a bruise;
Yet, loose one fibre, it may bleed to death.

DAVID

I have not loosed, nor will! Nay, I have grieved,
Bent down to human sympathy with you,
And hoarded tenderness you have not claimed,
To soothe you till you see. What can I more?
Take back the revelation and the law?
Reverse the advancing work, and, step by step,
Make all things as they were? I see your eyes

Lighten at this, as they had nigh forgot
To shine: I do believe you wish so much!

RHODA

(*Slowly.*)

No, no! Not if your happiness depends,—
Not less of power,—not all the work undone—
Oh, understand me, David!

DAVID

Patience, first!
Suspend your feeling till around us springs
The newer life, then judge if it be false.
But if, indeed, arises primitive peace,
And all that in the patriarchal years
Made manhood pure, and womanhood content,
Then I, by others, not of mine own faith,
Am justified to you.

SARAH

(*Entering.*)

Where have you put
Jonas, my husband? Give him back to me,
Or I will raise a tumult in the land!

DAVID

Your husband?

SARAH

Ay, and I'm his only wife.
You have him hidden: set him free, I say!

DAVID

Wild words are these. I know no more of him
Than those report who hear his discontent.
He hath not sought me; nor should I receive,
Unless he came with penitence.

SARAH

You *know*, —

I'll not believe you! Since he held to me,
Nor with strange women would pollute my house,
You mean his ruin! Help me, Prophet's wife!
Although, perverted by his tongue, you take
Your rival home —

[RHODA *starts, and turns away her face.*]

— yet you are woman still,
And my distress may somewhat touch your heart.
Find out what they have done with him, give back,
And we will go!

[*She weeps.*

DAVID

(*Aside*)

It is no acted fear:
Has he been taken? Is the answer come
To what I prayed, — come swiftly back to me

With all its helpless woe of consequence,
To make the wish a terror?

RHODA

In my heart
I feel your grief, and pity, and will help,
Can you but show the way.

DAVID

But I declare
Mine ignorance! I speak no further word,
Since you believe not.

SARAH

Nay, I will believe!
His fear was less of you than Nimrod Kraft,
Whose tongue — but that might anger if I spake:
I know not what to do!

DAVID

Why, go to him
Whom most you fear! But, stay! no evidence
Of evil in your frightened clamor lies.
Come with me, and confess the things you know.

[*Exit with her.*

RHODA

(*Solus.*)

Already? My prophetic heart declared,
Then called itself a liar! Not dare tell?
Such cowardice conceals a little love!
The winter sun, that for a distant land
Makes summer, cannot turn all warmth away,
And slowly comes again: let me not be
A frozen field, but gather every beam
He may allow me! Oh! I'll prove my right
By life or death; but now, on this alone,
I dare not brood. That woman, wild with fear,

And charged with reason for it, which alarms
Because unspoken — something lurks behind,
A further outrage to be sanctified,
A guilt thrust under David's innocence!
The thought confuses me: I only feel
The danger closing round us like a mist,
Cold, formless, chilling to the very bone;
And he is helpless, save I love him still.

ACT V.

SCENE I.

The street in front of the PROPHET'S *house.* PETER *at the gate, talking with two citizens.*

FIRST MAN

IT'S floating loose, as one might say: it comes
From everywhere and nowhere.

SECOND MAN

That's the way
To make things happen. Say they'll surely be,
And all the causes of them set to work.

FIRST MAN

I'd check; you'd let alone: which starts a cause,
Or hinders it? There's talk because there's fear.
What says the Prophet?

PETER

Nothing! If I asked,
And he should answer, something would be said;
But that we neither do.

SECOND MAN

Until he calls,
Confessing danger, in your pockets sheathe
Your restless hands, and whistle back your faith!
Their name is not yet Legion.

[*Exit.*

FIRST MAN

No, nor yours
A watchman of the Lord! There are no signs
Of Jonas yet; but people think him fled,
And plotting mischief in the enemy's camp.
The Twelve hold council: knowing these reports,
Which make alarm, they have not silenced them;
And thus suspicion grows.

PETER

I see it does.

FIRST MAN

You keep close-mouthed: I do believe you're primed
With far more knowledge than you let leak out.

PETER

I'm honest only: ignorance need not talk.

FIRST MAN

As I do, you would say?

[*Exit.*

PETER

He's in a huff,
But can't help counting me the wiser man.
Why, shut your mouth, and shrewdly move your head,

And stare right hard at him who speaks to you;
And, when he says, "It *is* so!" answer, "H'm,
Is it, indeed?" — and there's your capital
For thriving business in the wholesale trade
Of leading people. If I'd half a gift
To save from awkward usage of their minds,
I'd make them think me great.

RHODA

(*Coming from the house.*)

What have you heard?
This is no time for keeping back the truth.
There's danger somewhere.

PETER

One was sure of that,
The t'other not; but all I know is this, —
Some say the Gentiles mean to interfere,
Upset the Prophet's law, and him, the head,

Make chargeable for what the others do.
But that they can't: we're drifting on one raft;
And none but fools would ever try to take
The helmsman prisoner, till they smashed the crew.

RHODA

And all are faithful?

PETER

Well — they think they are.

RHODA

This was my fear: you mean that all are not?

PETER

It comes of management: the priest, and her —
Each is alone a match for any law;
And, if they work together —

RHODA

Nay, they *must!*
You are worse troubled than you care to show;
But I'll not question more. One way to help —
The hardest way that ever woman walked —
Is set before me, and I take it now!

[*Exit.*

PETER

I don't know as I'm gladder that she went,
Or sorrier that she seemed to think my wits
Of small account. Here's one that, as I guess,
She means to pump as deeply as he'll let.
He comes this way; he's got a blunted axe,
And I must turn the grindstone.

NIMROD

(*Entering.*)

Have you seen
Sarah, the wife of Jonas, pass this way?

PETER

Not I.

NIMROD

She still may come. Wait not for me,
Or any officer, but hold her fast!

PETER

There must be two of me, to do so much.

NIMROD

Large-boned, and strong of arm, she is, in fact.
You'll find a watchman yonder by the wood;
But scatter, lest she take another path!

PETER

Why, what's the row?

NIMROD

No more than you have heard.
Put what you know, and what you think might
be,

Together, and you'll find disturbance comes
Through her alone, and she can silence it.
The Prophet and the Twelve have that to ask,
Which, having answered, she disarmes herself.
[*Exit.*

PETER

No use of pumping there! The water comes
Just even with the spout, and then it stops.

SCENE II.

A room in LIVIA'S *house.*

LIVIA

(*Slowly pacing the floor, with a letter in her hand*).

Renounced, and half forgotten, still the world
Has power to hurt! I know the mirror false
Which makes a grim distortion of my face,
And yet it pains me while I look. What creed
Is theirs, to whom my love gives more offence,

Man's habit broken, than hath done my faith,
To them a fatal heresy of soul!
Those Pagans, to their monstrous idol bowed,—
Once Moloch named, but now Society,—
Defile, when turned to their forgotten Lord,
His altars with false fire. Ah! had I found
One pure male soul among them, not ashamed
To seek, believe, aspire, and overcome,—
With love's white heat to clarify my own,
And dear dependence on my differing force,—
I had remained! But thus, forbade to seek,
Insulted by insipid tenderness,
That into weakness fain would coddle power,
That shuts men's brains lest ours should be confused,
And hides strong aberrations of the sex,
Which, knowing, we might guide to purity,—
Why, what was left me but a fierce escape?
Thank Heaven, the line is passed! I've not to do

With threatened shame, or vain self-questioning,
more;
I give my being for a large return.

[*Enter* RHODA: *both stand for a moment, looking at each other, in silence.*]

Forgive me, Rhoda, if I show surprise;
Forgive me, also, that my doubt deterred
The due approach, which now your coming here
So gently chides!

RHODA

Do not mistake my heart,
Or set it lower, for the thing I do.
Save you perceive me as I verily am,
I cannot speak my message, or may mar.
I come, by sore necessity constrained,
Or I had never come.

LIVIA

(*Aside.*)

Her words awake
A new surprise: is this the fond, weak wife
I thought her, petulant instead of proud,
And simply sulking over fancied loss?

(*Aloud.*)

Your speech is bitterer, surely, than you mean;
But, seeming in the wrong, I must endure.

RHODA

Be not offended! I must needs suppose
Some curious resemblance in our hearts,
Else — yet it *must* be said! — you had not loved.
Let there be more, in this, — that, loving him,
You know no better service of your life
Than guarding his.

LIVIA

There read me by yourself!
I'll not explain my passion, since the words
Might sting with needless pangs. I thought you weak,
And find you strong: thus silence is enough.
You come because of him; forget the rest,
For partnership or rivalry in us
Has here one aim.

RHODA

I feel before I see,
And that which shakes me with continual dread
Dissolves when I would closelier scan its form.
The missing man, his wife's most real alarm,
The Gentile rumors, threatening David's place,
If not his freedom, and the ruin of all, —
These have a link which must be found and cleft.
Help me, therein: I am not quick of thought,

But I will follow, letting you direct.
You cannot, surely, unobservant be
Of each least danger, when you watch for him!

LIVIA

Less I may see, because I fear it less
Than you do. He must triumph as a chief,
Ere love can peacefully possess his life.
Unhelping there, love in its duty fails,
And all too anxiously may guard itself;
For opportunity wears danger's face
When first it comes; and now it may be so.
What you declare, I knew: I muse thereon,
To save, if the occasion shrinks to that;
But, if it broaden, to exalt as well!

RHODA

And you delay? to gain I know not what!
How can you thus so coldly, proudly talk

Of triumph won by risk? Ah! yes, I see
My heart's distress is folly unto yours:
I am a woman, and you know me not.
I show you all I dread; I give you chance
To set yourself above me in desert,
And on the remnant of my bliss to feed,
And you — seek "opportunity"!

[*She turns to leave.*

LIVIA

Not yet, —
You do mistake! and I should only wound
By picking words more nicely: all are edged
Which we two use. Twice have you made reproach,
Perhaps not meaning; I will let it pass,
And answer, since I pity your alarm,
With offered help: you may accept or leave.
How much of faith in Nimrod, the high-priest,
Do you preserve?

RHODA

(*After a pause.*)

If one's right hand could be
Unfaithful to the will? for so it seems.
But service, then, would measure treachery;
And that's too monstrous!

(*Aside.*)

Ah! what have I said?
Her words provoked the doubt I should conceal,
And this may do a mischief.

LIVIA

'Tis enough.
I know the thought, that, frightened, hides its face
Even from itself; but I will look on mine.
'Tis well you came to me: some sheltered plants
First note the distant changes of the air,
And here — the thing is possible: I thought

It might be later — Ha! if it be now,
I must to work!

RHODA

Give me a little part
When you have found it! so much is my right.

LIVIA

Ay, ay! I promise: now, I pray you, go!
For *his* sake, then!

[*Exit* RHODA.]

Oh! she may have her share;
But I, that dare and save and win and crown,
Shall sit by him as Zion's rightful queen!

Scene III.

The Council-Room. Nimrod, Simeon, *and* Mordecai *present.*

SIMEON

I find them more disturbed than timorous;
Still in good heart, the most: but that we keep
Continued silence, while the threats increase,
Bewilders them.

NIMROD

'Tis time, indeed, to act;
For our intent must be conveyed to all,
Or we shall fail in secret unity.
The Prophet halts: I've purposely left free
His spirit, praying for a path revealed
Where we, between the waves on either hand,
Dry-shod may walk: the revelation lags.
If unto me, less gifted, were transferred

The leader's office, I should exercise
With human wit, perchance, but also will
To wring success from stubborn circumstance.

SIMEON

Oh! were it so transferred! Can you not claim,
If we sustain you?

NIMROD

No, I will not claim!
What my devotion and obedience earn
Should I receive.

[*A knock is heard:* MORDECAI *goes to the door. As he opens it,* LIVIA *is seen.*]

(*Aside.*)

But to invite the trust,
So that the giver thinks he gives unasked,

Is always lawful. What she seeks is plain:
I've marked her keen ambition, and can use.

(*Aloud.*)

Admit the sister.

[LIVIA *comes forward to the table.*]

Opportunely come!
And hence the rules of council we suspend.
If you have knowledge, or your woman's wit
Works, with result, for our deliverance,
Be welcome, speak, and we shall gladly hear!

LIVIA

My knowledge is not more, my zeal not less,
Than yours; my skill to work with minor arts
Which must prevail with individual wills,
Ere, as a body, all are moved one way,
Perchance as great: so much is known to you.
This is no time for testing special power,
When any weapon, be it wielded well,

Becomes a rightful arm. Our danger lies
In suffering our young order to be jarred
Too suddenly, or slowly undermined
By such defence as leaves the end a doubt.
Between the two we need steer carefully.
You have the rudder; give an oar to me.

NIMROD

You apprehend the crisis, and have guessed
Why, measuring it, we have not spoken yet.
'Tis purposeless extremity of fear
Begets submission: what were best to do,
Too soon declared, is lightly criticised;
But, now they cry for guidance, we present
Calm fronts of unperturbed authority.
We crave to act: the Prophet only fails
In revelation, which may be denied,
If human craft suffice: or, unto you
Hath he declared his will?

LIVIA

Not unto me,
Surely, ungifted with commissioned power.

NIMROD

Yet that pretence of law which threatens us
Concerns you most. Our body is not yet
The giant it shall be: the covenant,
Now made an accusation, must be kept
By secret truth, the evidence held back,—
So, nothing proven, all their charges fail.
We best oppose by seeming to submit.
Unaided, they examine: not a tongue
Profanes the mysteries of Zion's house;
And, once so foiled, our skill and industry,
Our peace and order, only, noised abroad,
They will not haste to court a second blame.

SIMEON

The wisdom of the serpent speaks in that!

LIVIA

(*Aside.*)

And leaves the serpent's slime!

(*Aloud.*)

You, then, accept
Their whole procedure, — law, and court, and judge,
And twelve such fools as never heard of us,
Arrest, and trial? First, of course, they seize
The Prophet!

NIMROD

Me, instead! I will so lead
Suspicion from its present course in them.
My craft of brain, that cannot reach his gift
Of prayer and vision, hath its office here:
It will exalt my soul with holy joy
To triumph o'er the Gentiles!

LIVIA

Prophecy
Is that: the power awakes in you: I thought
Your gift was "craft of brain." Why, 'tis a scheme
Where every wheel must with a hundred *ifs*
Be cogged, or none of them will bite! The law
Takes any shape it likes: by prejudice
It moves the eleven, and wearies out the one
Within whose brain some dream of justice lives.
Yes, were our danger, law! But, while you wait
Your own arrest in all decorous form,
Whose hand shall stay the ruffian horde behind
From force and outrage?

NIMROD

Woman's brain is quick
To make a part the whole, and for her wits
Work easy triumph. I but told you part.

LIVIA

(*Aside.*)

Too quick, indeed! I should have cheated him
By feigned acceptance, till I learned the whole.
He may cajole by truth, as others do
By falsehood.

(*Aloud.*)

Nay, if hastily I spake,
The cause lay deeper than my woman's brain.

NIMROD

(*Smiling.*)

I saw it beating, faster than your words.
I but consider, not decide: the plan
Waits for the sanction of our Church's head,
Which he, in strange uncertainty, withholds.
If to the movement of his mind your own
May give direction, bid him not delay;

Or, still irresolute, set free my hands,
To work for him.

MORDECAI

The Twelve are as one man.

SIMEON

The priest speaks for us.

NIMROD

And the people wait.
Decide to help, where all is known and weighed;
Or, knowing little, work your random will,
And bring us ruin!

LIVIA

You would weigh me down
With much capacity. If you believed
My power, you would not threaten such result,
But coax and flatter me to shift my part.

Deal fairly, priest, and you shall have my aid!
You're certain of success: you only need
Unhindered leadership (the Prophet's place
Transferred, in seeming, that he 'scape the risk),
And then, submissive where they look for strife,
You will confound the Gentiles! Far too bold
For any brain but yours! Were not your blood
So passionless, your keen intelligence
So coldly watchful, I should doubt the end;
But now — I go to do the work you set!

[*Exit.*

MORDECAI

That's a beginning!

SIMEON

How you bent her will!
I never saw the like.

NIMROD

Ay, ay! The power
Sometimes is with me: may it oftener come!

(*Aside.*)

The work I set? She'll do the opposite,
Or else her lying candor lies again.
"So passionless!"—ha! ha! The time may come
When she shall say of me, "Too passionate!"
I think I've striven to turn away the storm;
But, if they will not see, so let it burst!
They're all mistaken: 'tis no thunder-cloud
That rattles half an hour, and rolls away;
But something that will tear us from our roots,
And sweep us far into the wilderness.
My own device might gain a little grace
To dull the blow: yet our prosperity
Tempts, as upon a counter scattered gold;
And, though the first wave strike us harmlessly,
A second one will follow. Better now
Set matters where they needs must terminate!
I've learned to rule, even while obeying most;
And I shall surely learn to bind and seal
By revelation, as my gifts increase.

Scene IV.

In front of the temple. A number of people collected; DAVID, NIMROD, and various members of the TWELVE, among them. LIVIA moves from one to another of the restless, excited groups.

A MAN

They should have armed us first!

A SECOND

The priest is shrewd
To keep his knowledge till it's time to use.
He has something ready: mark his quick gray eye!

A THIRD

The secrecy they lay upon us means
That we may be examined: more than that
It's hard to guess.

LIVIA

(*Whispering.*)

Keep you the peace, unless
They would arrest the Prophet, — then resist!

[*She passes on.*

A MESSENGER

(*To* DAVID.)

There are but four: their head is Sheriff Hyde.
Our watchmen stopped them at the wood below,
And now are leading hither: they would speak
With you, and with the Twelve.

DAVID

Go, bid them come!

NIMROD

Have you considered our united mind?
Here is it urgent that a single voice
Declare the answer.

DAVID

First must come demand,
Which, save its words and full intent were known,
We cannot meet beforehand. I will wait.

NIMROD

This only, let me speak! Exact delay
For consultation, when demand is made:
They are but four; yet each doth represent
A hundred more in ambush!

DAVID

Are you sure
Of Hugh's fidelity?

NIMROD

As of his life!
And whether Jonas did escape to them,
Or by the Lord was silenced, — either way

He served us first: so far have we been helped
To their discomfiture!

[*Movement in the crowd. The people fall back, and* COLONEL HYDE, *with three companions, guarded on each side by the watchmen of Zion, come forward.*]

COLONEL HYDE

Which man of you
Calls himself Prophet?

DAVID

Chosen of the Lord
Am I, and Prophet called by these, my flock.

COLONEL HYDE

You're he I seek. The law, that freedom gives
To manifold belief, now takes alarm
At vicious usages, by you proclaimed
As holy. You are called to meet the charge
Of wilful crime, with others, whom to this
You have persuaded.

[*Murmurs among the people.*]

DAVID

And should I resist
Such intermeddling with permitted faith?

COLONEL HYDE

Though loud report of your licentious lives
Commands my action, we are armed with proof,
And here resistance would be added crime.
Will you submit? or shall I raise my voice,
And call the County's power?

[*Tumultuous movement among the people.*]

VOICES

Go back! go back!
We guard the Prophet! Touch him if you dare!

NIMROD

Be quiet, brethren! Law should not be rash
To hasten conflicts which she might allay.

You, Colonel Hyde, have spoken: we demand
A space for counsel ere we make reply.
Come three days hence —

COLONEL HYDE

One day, no more!

[*Struggle and confusion on the outskirts of the crowd: mingled voices and cries.*]

SARAH

Let go!
I have done nothing! Let me free, I say!

DAVID

Hold, hold!

COLONEL HYDE

My cousin's wife!

SARAH

(*Rushing forward wildly, her hair streaming over her shoulders.*)

You have not seen
Jonas? No need to answer that: he's dead!
Oh, save me! take me with you!

NIMROD

(*Aside.*)

Curséd luck!
I thought she had escaped, but this is worse.

COLONEL HYDE

What means your terror?

SARAH

Jonas never came
From *you!* I thought him held, at first, and made
Vain outcries; then I feared for mine own life,
And hid till now. Upon my way to you

Came two, and held me fast with violent hands,
The Prophet's serving-man —

DAVID

It cannot be!
Peter?

SARAH

— and one the high-priest often calls
To do his secret work.

NIMROD

I ordered them.
The woman's grief, the Prophet's sympathy
Therewith, gave me desire to question her.
If thus our kindness frightens, let her go,
And you may test the value of the tongue
That speaks such folly!

COLONEL HYDE

Sarah, come with us!

(*To* DAVID.)

To-morrow, at this hour, expect me here!

[*Exit with* SARAH, *his companions, and the watchmen.*

NIMROD

(*Aside.*)

There go the Gentile torches, all ablaze,
Which shall consume the temple!

DAVID

Peter, here
If still you owe me service!

[*Exit.*

LIVIA

So, high-priest,
The court is opened, and the jury called;
Only the culprits have not reached the bar!

NIMROD

Some walls are built with clear design to stand
For ages; but the finger of a child
May pick a stone out ere the mortar dries,
And leave a crevice for the wedge of frost
To slowly split the fabric. You exult
As such a child might do.

LIVIA

(*Aside.*)

He frightens me!

Scene V.

Sunset. An outer street of the city. A number of men assembled: Peter *in the midst.*

SEVERAL VOICES

We will not yield!

A MAN

The Lord should send a sign,
If ever, now, when to His flock dismayed
The wolf comes howling!

PETER

'Tisn't just the howl.
He means to pounce upon our leader-ram,
Then lazily bite our throats from day to day.
The priest says, "Let him!" But you run down hill
To law, and up steep rocks climb out again.

VOICES

Ay, that is truth!

PETER

And he, to boot, mistakes
Through over-sharpness. Doing what he bade,

I harmed the Prophet in the sheriff's eyes;
And that wild woman will improve the tale,
Until they see — the Lord knows what — in him.
I'm bound to make my blunder good.

LIVIA

(*Approaching.*)

You are!
I'll show you how: there's little time to lose.
How many here have arms?

VOICES

I have! And I!

LIVIA

And, had you not the hearts of fighting men,
You would not answer thus. They think us weak
Or timorous: let them come in that conceit!
One sharp repulse will so confuse their plan

That time is gained; and what protection lies
In martial garrisons the nation plants,
For need, along the lawless, wild frontier,
May come to aid us, or to stand between.

VOICES

That's to the point! Such talk we understand.

LIVIA

Shall we submit to scarce the name of law,
Much less its substance? Who are they that shake
The sword of justice, which would pierce themselves
If they let go the hilt? What! suffer them
To seize at will, until our strength is shorn,
And Zion's riches to their hands lie bare?
Not you! I know you!

VOICES

No, we'll fight them first!

LIVIA

You will! And, if no man dares lead you forth,
I'll be your captain: there are Jaels yet!
Let each his neighbor summon; scour your guns,
Run even your clock-weights into bullet-moulds,
And tell your wives that milk from manly veins
Looks worse than blood!

[*She beckons to one of the men following her, who comes forward, and unrolls a banner, with a golden lion on a red ground.*]

Behold our banner spread,
Yours and the Prophet's! See that first it float
Amid the smoke, which, when it drifts away,
Leaves victory behind! You want a song,
To set the courage of your hearts in words,

And bid it ring beneath the echoing heaven.
Hear, then! I've made it for you, and will sing!

[*She sings.*]

Children of Zion,
Crouch as a lion,
Eager to fly on
  Foes that deride!
Rise for the Prophet!
Arm for the Prophet!
Fight for the Prophet!
  Fling his banner wide!

ALL

(*Enthusiastically repeating the last lines, as chorus.*)

Fight for the Prophet!
  Fling his banner wide!

[*The men gradually disperse.*]

LIVIA

(*Solus.*)

I live at last! 'Twas more than love inspired
This counter-plot, though love like mine were more

Than cause and needful spur. I live and move,
Bid others live and play the parts I set,
Concentrate petty forces to one end
Which grandly must succeed, or grandly fail, —
But, either way, I act! The top of life,
Methinks, is action, when the field is broad;
For power of nature cannot truly be,
Till it is proved on others.

Ah, he comes!

My dream was that I work for him alone:
Why, since both power and passion wed, I do!

[DAVID *approaches.*]

Lift up your front, my Prophet! 'Tis the eve
Of strength secured: the test, the hostile charge,
Draw near the moment when they sink in dust;
And, after one dim bar of cloud, your sun
Will hold the sky!

DAVID

'Tis dusk: the sun is down.
Old habit says the day will dawn again
After a certain darkness: have you thought,
What if it should not dawn? 'Tis possible.

LIVIA

Yes, when no triumph calls the daylight up;
When human souls, in all God's world, are dumb;
When hope is choked, and, like neglected fire,
The spark of prayer dies out, and even love
Awaits no morrow sweeter than to-day, —
Then, then, 'twere possible!

DAVID

Can light be drawn
Even from the spirit, as the warmth from blood?
You seem to shine, as you possessed the glow
I thought was mine: you see where I am dark;

And, where I walk confounded, you rejoice.
Whence comes your confidence? What near success
Fore-glorifies you?

LIVIA

Pardon, if to you
I still keep silent! Faith, no less than love,
May have its budded secret, soon to bloom.
For some few rapid hours endure your place,
As now, while others work, — I least, perhaps,
Though most in will: the lower necessity
Is ours to meet, yea, ours to overcome.

DAVID

They wait my word.

LIVIA

I know it. They best learn
Now, when their minds are sore perturbed, to wait.
Can you bestow on clouded eyes and brains

Your perfect gift? or justify each step,
Greater than Moses, to the murmuring throng?
The human with the godlike essence strives
In you; and, when your soul would sanction straight,
The heart stands up in protest: heed it not,
While others can be merely man!

DAVID

Go, then!
I cannot meet your words, and will not ask
What hope sheds brightness on your face. Farewell!

LIVIA.

Farewell!

[*Exit* DAVID.]

And for the last time, half-apart
And half-acknowledged, do I say, Farewell!

Scene VI.

Night. A room in the Prophet's *house.* David, *seated at a desk, with his back towards* Rhoda. *He opens papers, looks at them mechanically, lays them aside, and at last rests his head upon his hand.* Rhoda *sits in another part of the room, with her hands clasped in her lap. Once or twice she lifts her head, looks at* David, *and seems about to speak.*

DAVID

(*Turning suddenly.*)

You're watching me!

RHODA

Nay, waiting, and, besides,
Wishing that you would speak. To-day's affairs
Leave me in doubt of what the morrow brings.
There's something in a charge that frightens me,
Though vilely made: I never dreamed that crime,
Even as a painted threat, could be so flung
Into our faces.

DAVID

Into mine, not yours!

RHODA

It is the same: the threat, the impossible fact,
One like the other, at my honor strikes.
I do not think of that. Oh, were the day,
And all its horrible aspects, safely o'er!
Were you a nameless servant of the Lord,
Somewhere with me and with our helpless child,
A taper burning calmly, not, as now,
A bonfire whirled and beaten by the winds,
What peace were mine!

VOICES

(Outside, singing in passing.)

Fight for the Prophet!
Fling his banner wide!

RHODA

But, no! you dare not fly,
Though yet the chance is free. The frightened flock,
In its devoted faith, appeals to you,
Who, having led to this, must lead beyond.
An hour's enough: the river's middle stops
Pursuit and summons; but, were you and I
This moment seated on the farther shore,
We needs must cross again.

DAVID.

Do you say that?
Do you set duty higher than our lives?
Why, she could say no more!

RHODA

(In a low voice.)

Ah, spare me, David!

[*A long silence.*]

DAVID

(*Musingly.*)

Were we together, Rhoda? yes, we were!
One day in June; long, long ago it was:
Wild strawberries along the clearing's edge
Were thick that year; but we grew tired at last;
And I, stretched flat among the fragrant vines,
Looked at the sky: I saw no other thing.
The blue retreated as my vision reached;
And as a pebble slowly deeper, deeper sinks
In still, dark water, up and upward sank
My soul, and sank, and still there was no end.
Somewhere, at last, beyond the invisible stars,
A hoary brightness gathered from the void,
And from the midst there looked a single Eye,
Compact of all ineffable light, — His eye!
And did not blind me.

RHODA

David! and I cried:
You would not speak: I thought you vexed, unkind!
I could not know, till now.

DAVID

We came from school
One day, when, from a rising arch of cloud,
The tempest strained the black-oak on the hill.
You feared to pass: I shouted, through the roar,
"You will not hurt us, God!" and then a bolt
Split with red fire the surging firmament.
But you were pale with terror; on my breast
You hid your eyes; while I, in solemn joy,
Chanted aloud, and waved my arms aloft,
And felt strange fingers pluck my beaten hair,
As one may tease in fondness. Say, do you
Remember, Rhoda?

RHODA

(*Weeping.*)

Oh, I do!

DAVID

How now,
You cry for memory of it? Ah! I see,
Your memory wears another hue than mine.
You tremble: I exult!

RHODA

Upon us sweeps
A blacker tempest now.

DAVID

Go you to rest;
If struggle come, so gather strength for it.
Fret not for me: my body must be as dead
Before my soul is verily alive.

[*Exit* RHODA, *slowly.* *A pause.*]

They look to me: if I, in turn, look up,
What help is certain? Yea, but first to look!
I urge my thought; but, swerving from its aim,
It backward speeds, and paints anew the past
In colors which confound me. 'Tis not doubt;
'Tis no renewal of old agonies:
But something cold, that wears the shape of Truth,
Treads down with heavy step, along my path,
The springing harvest, and with fateful hand
Makes sign, "Go on: I follow!"

Get you gone,
Device of Satan! To His law a lie?
He made the covenant a perfect chain,
Which, link by link, am I restoring, soon

To girt us round about, — a lesser world
Where He may reign: one flaw, and all must
go!
One flaw? There is no torture known in hell
Enough for such malevolence, if so!
I'll put Thee to the test: our strait is sore;
Thine intervention, since the world began,
Never so needed: do Thy miracle!
Or stand aloof, and let Thy thunders growl
In leash, Thy lightnings flash a distant threat;
But breathe one word of counsel, — give my soul,
Passive before Thee, one victorious thought!

[*He paces the room for some minutes in great excitement, then suddenly stops.*]

My prayers rebound, as from a solid wall;
My brain refuses to anticipate
The coming problem; and my very hope
Strains, like an eye in darkness, foiled of use!

What palsy thus disorders every sense
Wherein the spirit lives? I cannot see
A hand's-breadth forward, nay, nor fancy aught:
The light burns backward over what has been;
And its last glimmer, fading at my feet,
Leaves all the future darkness!

Oh, my God!
The mortal anguish of a life at bay,
Escape cut off, the certainty of doom,
All that is visited upon the flesh, —
Methinks were easy. Mine is death in life;
The sinews severed, and the strength as dead;
No power to reach, not even knowledge left
Of how or whither, but the soul a corpse!
I'll strive no more; I'll neither think nor
pray:
Let accident become my deity!

SCENE VII.

The interior of the Temple. Men, women, and children gathered in groups. NIMROD, *on the platform in front of the Holy of Holies, trims the lights burning in the seven-branched candlesticks.* SIMEON *and* MORDECAI, *near the door, conferring with two messengers.*

FIRST MESSENGER

I counted them as they came o'er the rise,
And nigh two hundred were they.

SIMEON

Did you mark
Some in advance? — signs of a summons first,
Preceding force?

FIRST MESSENGER

Their march was orderly.

SIMEON

(*To* MORDECAI.)

Then it would seem he has them well in hand;
And, whether violence be done, depends
Chiefly on him. But who went forth from us?

SECOND MESSENGER

This side the border brook, I saw go out
Three Members of the Twelve: John surely was
The first, Elisha and Zerubbabel
I thought the others.

MORDECAI

(*To* SIMEON.)

By the Prophet sent?

SIMEON

By him allowed; for neither Yea nor Nay
He answered them or me. His gifts grow weak

When most we need them; but the day may cast
The power in stronger hands, and save us all!

[*Sound of drums and trumpets outside. Voices singing.*]

Fight for the Prophet!
Fling his banner wide!

SIMEON

Hark, there! Who leads them? Follow,—bring report!

[*Exit Messengers.*

NIMROD

(*Coming down from the altar.*)

My hands are tied: all ye who hear me note!
Bear witness, that, if blood be shed this day,
My garments are not stained. I would have given
Myself as pledge, so using human craft
(Which, for His glory, sanctifies the Lord)
To foil the Gentiles; now it seems too late;

But, when all other virtue is outworn,
Then turn to me.

WOMEN

Go forth, and hold them back!

NIMROD

Though driven to ruin's edge, I still obey:
Heed ye the lesson!

[*Enter* DAVID *pale and troubled:* RHODA *follows him, bearing the child in her arms.*]

DAVID

(*Looking on the frightened groups.*)

Save all these, high-priest!
I give them to your hands: take boat, and cross
Beyond the reach of this authority
Which smites them with disorderly alarm.
'Twill soon be settled whether you return,
Or we must join you.

NIMROD

Suffer me to wait,
While aught of peril menaces yourself!

[*Sounds of firing in the distance: cries and confusion among the people.*]

A MAN

(*Rushing in.*)

They're firing, by the wood! Theirs, on the plain;
Ours, covered by the timber: some were down
Before the smoke got thick!

DAVID

(*To* MORDECAI.)

It must not be!
Quick! — something white! Within the chancel, there,
My prophet-mantle, as the sign of truce!

[*While* MORDECAI *obeys this command, the sound of firing draws nearer.*]

PETER

(Enters, wounded in the arm.)

First, give me water.

[*It is brought from the baptismal font. He drinks.*]

Scarce there's time to tell:
Get over the river! — that was what she said.

DAVID

Who brought this on?

PETER

They wanted you, — no less
Would answer: we refused to give you up,
And blocked their marching nearer; then — they fired!
Our volleys tore and scattered them a bit,
But they're too many. She went here and there,
Put heart in all, and like a general led,

And not a bullet touched her: then, when I
Was hit in turn, she sent me posting here.
We're falling back, but slowly, facing them:
Don't lose a minute — ugh! the thing's no fun:
My arm feels ugly.

[*He faints.*]

DAVID

Rhoda, look to him!
My place is at the front: 'tis me alone
They seek, and they may have me!

[*Exit.*

RHODA

(*Giving her child to one of the women.*)

Lift his head,
Undo his collar! There! I've bound his arm,
And bathed his brow with water from the font:

He soon will breathe again. I pray you, give
My child your tenderness, if I should die!

[*Exit, following* DAVID.

NIMROD

You heard? He gave you to my hands: I charge,
By him commissioned, that your fears be still!
If there be traitors here, let flame from Heaven
Their tongues make cinder, that they cannot speak!
We will submit, in all external forms,
Even to the Gentiles; then in secret pass
The river, bearing our most precious goods
Beyond their reach: our spies have gone abroad,
And found another Eshcol in the West.
Within our hands lies all we builded here,
And they, upheld by faith, shall build again!
This is no time for lamentation: hope
As ye have never hoped, have confidence
Ye never felt, await triumphant signs
Reserved for you, His people!

VOICES

Yea, we will!

[*Scattered musket-shots outside the temple: wild, piercing cries are heard. Immediately afterwards the chancel-door is torn open, and a number of armed men, some of them wounded, enter the temple. Then* DAVID *appears, shot through the breast, and held up by* RHODA *and* LIVIA, *supporting him on either side. Cries and lamentations among the people gathered in the temple.*]

DAVID

Forward! to the altar, to the altar!

CRIES

Lord!
Save him, Thy Prophet, for Thyself and us!

[DAVID, *supported by* RHODA *and* LIVIA, *totters forwards, and is upheld by them, leaning against the altar.*]

DAVID

Oh for a little life! it fades so fast!
Hear me, my brethren! I will only speak
Words needful: not too late, the shadow falls
That veiled mine eyes: confusion has an end.

NIMROD

(*Aside.*)

What means he?

(*Aloud, to the people.*)

Silence, all! The Prophet speaks,
In this extremity, to you!

DAVID

(*With difficulty.*)

Be still!
Each word you utter steals a word of mine,
And few are left me: let me but begin!
I see so much at once! all things are clear;

But speech grows weak. Ah, hearken, brethren
mine!
How say it all? I pray you, bid your souls
Rise quickly up, and save me half! O God,
It is for Thee! Leave me one moment here!
See, I am dying! On the edge of life,
Truth's lightning flashes backward and beyond:
So hear! First— Hold me firm, I slide away!
Lord, Lord, be merciful! no time is left!
I see no more — but, yes! one blesséd face:
'Tis yours! — you're with me, Rhoda! — *you*, my
love!

[*He turns towards* RHODA *as he speaks, and falls upon her breast, with his arms hanging over her shoulders.*]

LIVIA

Help! Lift him up! he faints.

RHODA

Nay, he is dead!
Leave us! You have no more a part in him:
He is all mine at last!

[*Clasping* DAVID *to her breast, she sinks slowly down at the foot of the altar.*]

NIMROD

So death cuts short
The weakness which has nigh betrayed us all!
His gift and power become our heritage;
And Zion lives, and shall be strong, through me!

[COLONEL HYDE *and his men force an entrance into the portal of the temple. A wild scene of confusion among the people.* NIMROD KRAFT *snatches the ark from the altar, and escapes through the chancel-door.*]

THE CURTAIN FALLS.

www.ingramcontent.com/pod-product-compliance
Lightning Source LLC
LaVergne TN
LVHW010215110826
845151LV00004B/1088

* 9 7 8 1 4 2 5 5 2 8 4 1 6 *